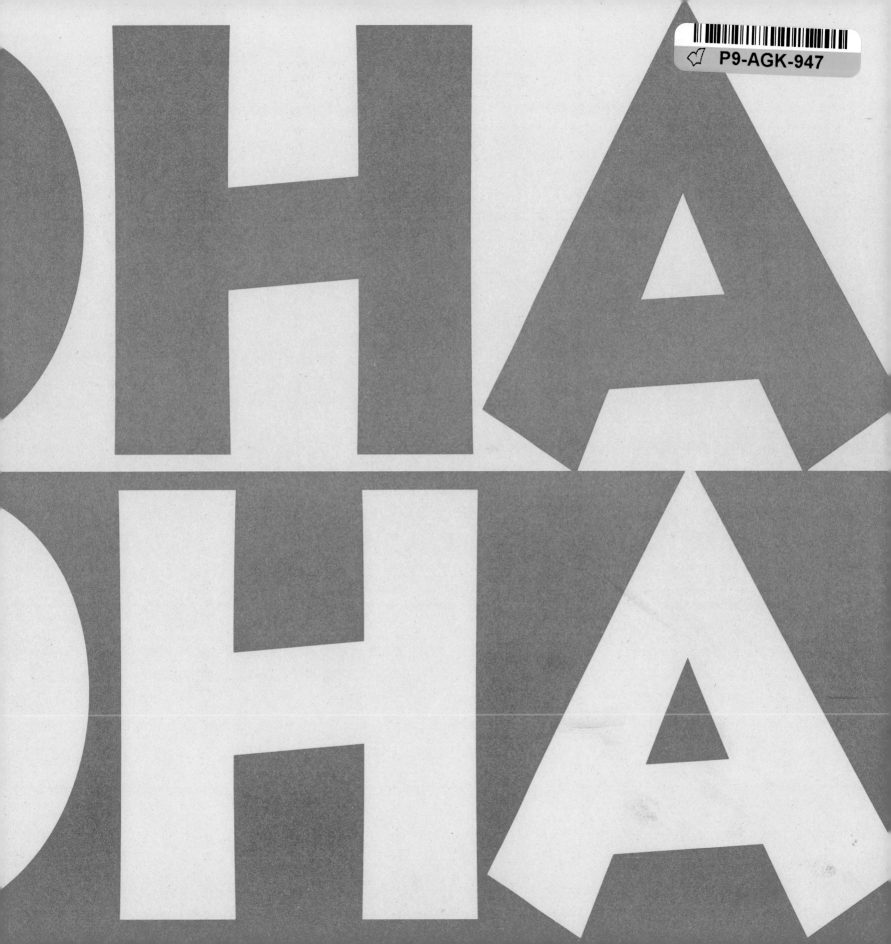

P9-AGK-947

The Islands of

HAWAII

KAUAI · NIIHAU · OAHU · MOLOKAI · LANAI · MAUI · KAHOOLAWE · HAWAII

UNDER THE
HULA MOON

UNDER THE HULA MOON
Living in Hawai'i

Jocelyn Fujii

**PHOTOGRAPHS BY
LINNY MORRIS CUNNINGHAM**

FOREWORD BY PAUL THEROUX

DESIGN BY KEN SANSONE

CROWN PUBLISHERS, INC. / NEW YORK

Mahalo to the following contributors: Sheila Donnelly and Associates, Dollar Rent a Car, Hawaii Visitors Bureau, Stouffer Waiohai Beach Resort.

And special consultants: DeSoto Brown, Charles K. L. Davis, Phyllis Fox and the Historic Hawai'i Foundation, Spencer Leineweber, Glenn Mason, May Moir, Linda O'Connor, Nalani Olds, Tyrone Reinhardt, Don Severson, Hannah Springer, Ray Wong.

Grateful acknowledgment is made to *The Atlantic* and Brandt & Brandt Literary Agents, Inc., for granting permission to reprint an excerpt from an article by Kathryn C. Hulme that appeared in the January 1965 issue of *The Atlantic Monthly*.

Copyright © 1992 by Jocelyn Fujii
Foreword copyright © 1992 by Paul Theroux
Photographs copyright © 1992 by Linny Morris Cunningham

Photograph credits: page 2, 3 (right) by DeSoto Brown; 19 (top), from the Meck Collection, Bishop Museum; 30 (bottom) by Werner Stoy, Bishop Museum; 174, 175 (top) by J. D. Griggs, U. S. Geological Survey; 175 (bottom) copyright © by Franco Salmoiraghi.

All rights reserved. No part of this book may be reproduced or transmitted in any form or by any means, electronic or mechanical, including photocopying, recording, or by any information storage and retrieval system, without permission in writing from the publisher.

Map on page 1 courtesy Lahaina Printsellers and Steve Strickland. Bas relief on page 142 by Roy Venters.

Styling by Linny Morris Cunningham and Mark Cunningham.

Published by Crown Publishers, Inc., 201 East 50th Street, New York, New York 10022. Member of the Crown Publishing Group. CROWN is a trademark of Crown Publishers, Inc.

Manufactured in Japan

LIBRARY OF CONGRESS
CATALOGING-IN-PUBLICATION DATA

Fujii, Jocelyn K.

Under the hula moon: living in Hawaii / Jocelyn Fujii.

Includes bibliographical references and index.
1. Hawaii—Description and travel.
2. Hawaii—Social life and customs.
3. Hawaii—Pictorial works. I. Title.
DU623.25.F85 1992
996.9'04—dc20   92-7176

ISBN 0-517-58131-0

10 9 8 7 6 5 4 3 2 1

FIRST EDITION

For his fierce heart
and innocent compassion,
I am indebted
to Bradley Shields.
This book is dedicated
to him.

Contents

FOREWORD *by Paul Theroux* / 8

INTRODUCTION / 12

Hawai'i **THEN** / 17

KAMA'ĀINA / 33

PLANTATION / 55

PANIOLO / 75

MAKAI / 95

MAUKA / 113

The **GARDEN** / 129

CONTEMPORARY Style / 143

Rooms That Tell a **STORY** / 157

The **VAGABOND'S** House / 163

Glossary / 176

Bibliography / 177

Acknowledgments / 178

Index / 179

FOREWORD *by Paul Theroux*

I never thought much about living on islands until I came to Hawai'i. Why was this? I had lived on many islands in the past—in Singapore, on Martha's Vineyard, around the archipelago of Great Britain. But Hawai'i inspired me and gave me hope, and I began to understand "rock fever," the condition of being an islander. In Hawai'i I felt I was always half outdoors, which was where I wanted to be—nature mattered. And I was constantly reminded of where I was. I felt very lucky.

A person inhabiting a house on an island can seem rather special. Such people may have left the mainland in a spirit of renunciation and in quest of anonymity, but houses on islands, and islanders too, can seem as conspicuous in life as in fiction. Obviously, that is part of the fun of island living—the high profile, the romance, the gossip, the inbreeding. It would be hard to overestimate any islander's taste for drama.

Literature is a good guide to island style. So often, an island in a book stands for the whole world. Look at *Robinson Crusoe* or *Lord of the Flies*, or the greatest of all island tales, Shakespeare's *The Tempest*. Prospero's island contains just about all the moods and characters one associates with any island—not merely remoteness and a powerful spirit life, but magic and wonderment as well as instantly familiar folk. Most Hawaiians would quickly recognize Caliban as a so-called local, Prospero as a *kama'āina* (an old-timer), and the rest of the cast as *malihinis* (newcomers).

An island's solitariness gives it its importance. I wonder if the Falklands would have been quite so stoutly defended if they had been the foreshore of a continent. They are depicted in the

popular mind as a microcosm of British society overrun by a pack of unruly Latins. It is rare in fiction for an island not to be an even more complex microcosm, the world in miniature, the smallest possible geographical entity, but containing everything. Conditioned this way, the people who choose to live on islands regard themselves as having entered paradise.

Greenland is an island, and so is Australia, but in these cases it is purely a technical description. Usually when we think of islands the image that comes to mind is a small, pretty piece of land surrounded by a watery wilderness, a metaphor for isolation—indeed, a metaphor for life itself. "To be born is to be shipwrecked upon on island," one of my characters says in my novel *The Family Arsenal*, quoting, I think, Walter de la Mare.

"I was born on a dot in the ocean," V. S. Naipaul once said to me, referring dismissively to Trinidad. His lack of sentiment is rare among islanders. A Hawaiian from the island of Kaua'i told me sadly of her

first journey to the mainland at the age of fifteen, and she said she found the trip bittersweet. "It was as though I was losing my innocence." The way she described it made it sound like an expulsion from paradise. And Kaua'i might well be paradise—isn't the whole point of an island its uniqueness as a place apart, existing outside the world? Even the tamest nearest island—Staten Island and the Isle of Wight spring to mind—has a distinct character. And no one travels to an island casually—there is always an element of drama in such a trip. Even the ferry passengers leaving Woods Hole for the island of Martha's Vineyard—only an hour away and usually visible—even

these daytrippers are put in a mood and begin to reflect on the poetry of departure.

But Alcatraz is an island, and Devil's Island is part of the popular horror imagery of abandonment. Thematically they represent only imprisonment and they are exclusively punitive. I once canoed to an island in the middle of Lake Nyasa (as it was called twenty-five years ago) and was attacked by crazy monkeys. The monkeys had been exiled there because they had been such a nuisance to a particular village. Why no one had killed them I cannot imagine, because the monkeys were very fierce and rather murderous-looking themselves. They snatched at my head and made rushes at me from trees; I beat them back with a stick and then—breathless and scared—paddled away. But it was a good example of the effectiveness of an island prison, particularly for a nonswimming species.

Classically a person goes to an island in much the same spirit a person heads into exile—seeking simplicity, glorying in a world that is still incomplete and therefore full of possibilities. Anything can happen on an island—guilt can be expiated (*Robinson Crusoe*); the forces of good and evil can emerge in the breasts of castaways (*Lord of the Flies*); love can be discovered (*The Blue Lagoon*); so can a great fortune (*Treasure Island*) or a true paradise (Melville's *Typee*) or a kind of hell (Conrad's *Victory*); it can be the setting for a great departure (the Nantucket of *Moby*

Dick) or the oddest landfall on earth (*Gulliver's Travels*). Reality has been stranger than those fictions—not only Robert Louis Stevenson living out the fantasy of high chieftainship in Samoa, or Napoleon waiting in the wilderness of St. Helena, Darwin understanding natural selection in the Galapagos, and the true language of Scotland living on undamaged in the Outer Hebrides, but more recently those Japanese soldiers, strange leftovers from World War II emerging from Pacific islands, still armed and willing to fight for the emperor. It is impossible to imagine these island episodes occurring on the mainland.

The common denominator is not the landscape of the island or its location on the globe, but rather the fact of a place being surrounded by water. The character of water itself is the magic element, offering the islander transformation. This is the beginning of the emergence of island style, too.

The water, seemingly nothing, is everything—a moat, a barrier, a wilderness, the source of food and hope, the way out; the ocean—as any true seagoing person will testify—is a place. It has specific moods and locations, as any landscape of hills and valleys does. I was paddling a kayak this past winter in Cape Cod, off Great Island—

which is a "neck" rather than a true island—and saw a man standing up to his waist in Lewis Bay, thrashing around with some traps. He was happy to greet a passerby on this freezing day and he told me he was an oyster fisherman setting out his cages. This seems a happy and harmless occupation until you learn that oysters are often harvested in the millions by one person and because of a scarcity they fetch fifty cents each. Anyway, this potential millionaire in rubber waders described himself as an "aquaculturist," and he gestured at the black waters of the bay and said, "I am leasing these five acres." The Polynesian sailor similarly sees the ocean as an extension of the land and knows where he is from the character of the waves or the swell as much as from the stars. The Pacific is full of ancient named waterways—the paths to other islands or archipelagos. A stretch of water in Hawai'i is called Kealaikahiki, The Way to Tahiti (twenty-five hundred miles away). But this is a subtle business, because water gives the ideal illusion of emptiness—while appearing to be nothing, it is everything and contains all possibilities.

I don't say that every islander recognizes this. There is, for example, the mental condition called "rock fever"—the need to leave an island. But another kind of rock fever must lead a person back to the island. It is easy enough to conceive the notion that your island is a sort of fortress. Or, to change the image, the island may represent the most formidable sort of seagoing vessel, a kind of battleship.

Boat owners find islands and settle on them. That is the pattern. And the boat owner's mentality—the skipper's mind-set—is the

islander's characteristic way of thinking. Typically it includes self-sufficiency, having things your own way, making your own rules, expecting to be obeyed, establishing conventions, and developing your own style. Such a person has a history—he may be fleeing a situation or wishing to make a new life—but in any case it is hard to think of an islander and not

think of Robinson Crusoe or Prospero, just as it is impossible to think of a native islander and not think of Caliban or Friday. Islomaniacs tend to believe that it is possible for them to control their own lives on an island, as nowhere else. I think this is probably a delusion, but even so it is one that has led many people to cast themselves off from the mainland and seek the fastness of an island. So often they go believing that they are bestowing something on the island, but the reverse of this is much more common, and they are possessed.

Long before he discovered the Pacific, and while he was still in Edinburgh, Stevenson wrote:

> *I should like to rise and go*
> *Where the golden apples grow;*
> *Where below another sky*
> *Parrot islands anchored lie.*

I think many people entertain the same notion and would agree with him. The trouble is that not all of us with that in mind can fulfill this fantasy. That is why we find people creating islands where there is no water—it is the reason for the house in the woods, the house surrounded by wilderness, the house on the prairie. And what is the penthouse suite in a skyscraper if not a metropolitan effort to create the illusion of an island in the density of a cityscape? It is the motive behind the creation of a great lawn, with a house at its center; and the house on the hill is also an island fantasy.

Obviously, the person who emigrates to an island is different from the native islander. It strikes me that there is something rather suspect about a person who seeks to recapture island innocence. But in any case it is a futile search, because no one really can take possession of an island. Being the monarch of all you survey is in reality a mainland conceit; on an island it is you who are possessed. Islands seem to have a unique capacity to take hold of their inhabitants, whether they be natives or castaways or potential colonizers, and that is perhaps why island mythology is so rich.

Seventy years after they were studied in detail by Malinowski, the Trobriand Islands are pretty much unchanged. I have been paddling in that island group (which is on the northeast coast of Papua New

Guinea) in my collapsible kayak, and I am happy to report that Malinowski's *The Sexual Life of Savages*—in spite of its patronizing title—is still an accurate account of life today, down to the last flourish of free love during the yam festival. Neither the Mormons nor the Seventh Day Adventists have effected much of a change in traditional sexual mores, and it would be hard to find a happier, more energetic people anywhere in the Pacific.

The Trobrianders are building seagoing canoes much as they were when Malinowski described them in *Argonauts of the Western Pacific*. They worship the same gods and live in fear of the same witches. They are brilliant and ingenious fishermen and sailors; they are resourceful and successful gardeners. They are lucky enough to be living on coral islands that are not only very remote but also invisible until you are a mile or so offshore. I suppose it is only a matter of time before the Japanese decide to introduce the Trobrianders to the jet ski. (It goes almost without saying that the Japanese themselves are the epitome of the most paranoid sort of islanders, espousing racial purity, intense xenophobia, and a fortress mentality.)

But these are generalities. More remarkable are the unique traits of different islands and islanders. One only has to consider Venice, Singapore, Zanzibar, and the holy island of Lindisfarne to see that what they have in common is a great deal less significant than each one's distinct identity. Even Nantucket and Martha's Vineyard, seemingly so close—I have paddled from one to the other in less than a day—are quite different both in landscape and in character, the Vineyard being an easily reachable offshore island of hills and woods and meadows, entirely inhabited by celebrities, and Nantucket something else again —a windswept and duney moorland, far enough in the Atlantic to be beneath the horizon, to be cut off in storms, and this remoteness, and its fogs and winds, has given Nantucket a genuinely spooky character. I think the same is true of the Blasket Islands off the Irish coast—they are so much themselves and so unlike the Dingle Peninsula across the

water; and Ramsay Island off St. David's Head on the coast of Wales seemed to me actually dangerous—and un-Welsh— though there was little else on it but falcons and the ruins of the huts of hermit monks.

An island ought to seem fragile and isolated, and yet I have never seen one or lived on one that did not seem like a complete thing itself, self-contained and self-sufficient because of the surrounding water. Whether this is an illusion or not I don't know, but this sense of mystery and power must communicate itself both to those who are native to the islands and those who seek them. There is something princely in the very situation of someone who builds a house on an island and lives in it. It is both a principate and the ultimate refuge—a magic and unsinkable world.

INTRODUCTION

There are many ways of living in Hawai'i.

You can live in a tent, a mansion, a chic downtown high-rise, a quonset hut, an upcountry ranch, a hundred-year-old plantation home, a surfer's shack, a mountain retreat with an English garden. You can live at ocean's edge, in a stream of salutary salt air, or in the heights, where the northeasterly trade winds whirl through the ridgetops before descending to cool the lowlands.

Wherever you are in Hawai'i, you are on an island, on a finite land mass with north and south shores, a windward and a leeward side. You can ski on Mauna Kea at more than thirteen thousand feet and snorkel an hour later in the warmest waters in the state. Lava tubes may hiss and steam only a few feet from the shoreline, and waterfalls stream down the flanks of dormant, desertlike volcanoes. In Hawai'i, these microclimates vary more in a short distance than in most places on earth.

On the eight major islands of Hawai'i—seven of them populated—live 1,108,000 Islanders who thrive in this diversity. Generations removed from the original Polynesian settlers (said to have arrived around 500 to 750 A.D.), the missionaries who came in the nineteenth century, and the sugar barons who spawned the influx of immigrant laborers, contemporary Islanders still represent a healthy mix of all that came before them. Their tastes, styles, foods, customs, and homes reflect this hybrid quality, while their faces tell the story of a racial melding that has not ebbed since the 1800s. As irrevocably westernized as Hawai'i is, it remains multiethnic to its core.

Whether newcomer, *kama'āina*, easterner, westerner, urbanite, country folk, young, or old, those who have made Hawai'i their home share a common isolation that places them twenty-five hundred miles from the nearest continent. The ocean is the womb and the horizon a reminder of their self-chosen exile. *Mauka*—toward the mountain—and *makai*—toward the sea—are the primary orientations. The backdrop for their lives may be a desert, a rain forest, the shoreline, the heights—even the tumultuous reaches of an active volcano.

As I write this, a sea of molten lava is surging to the sea on the island of Hawai'i. It has mowed down—buried—the village of Kalapana, adding more than 180 structures to its list of casualties. Now covered with layers of lava, fabled attractions have fallen to the fury of the volcano goddess Pele: the National Park Visitors' Complex at Waha'ula, the beloved Queen's Bath bathing pool, and, most recently, the black-sand beach of Kaimu. Every day for months the tally has risen: 117 homes destroyed by lava, then 125, then 136, and, at present, 182 buildings lost since the eruption of Kīlauea Volcano began in 1983. Pouring from a vent, through underground lava tubes, and then creeping, inch by inch, toward the sea, the lava has left in its wake only memories of Kalapana and the good times enjoyed by families and surfers at the two-hundred-year-old black-sand beach.

No one can imagine the feelings of these volcano-area residents, who have eked out a life and made green things grow on arid stretches of black, inhospitable lava. Like the ferns, 'ōhi'a, 'ōhelo, and other pioneer plants that sprout from the hardened magma, it's Hawai'i's latter-day

pioneers who have greened these lands and lost their homes and their dreams there. More than anything else in Hawai'i, the destruction of a home by lava underscores the fundamental difference between Hawaiians, who traditionally believe they are stewards of the land, and westerners, who subscribe to the notion of ownership.

The early Hawaiians had a land-based culture, yet had no concept or practice of private land ownership until the westerners arrived. Millions of Americans watched on television as a mainlander, a part-time Island resident, vented his anger after lava overran his home in what he had supposed was the Aloha State. In the same devastated subdivision of Kalapana, a Hawaiian woman who had raised thirteen children there watched calmly as the molten mass approached, giving thanks for the privilege of raising her children on a patch of earth that belonged to Pele. Here and there at the front of the lava flow or at the rim of an accessible crater, bundles of *ti* leaves contain the offerings of Islanders honoring their mythology in living form. Ask any Hawaiian who has lost his home in the awesome devastation of the volcano, and a typical response would be: "This land belongs to Pele, and it's hers to take back if she wants to. We thank her for letting us stay here. And then we move up *mauka* [toward the mountain]." The attitude is beyond stoicism; it reflects the inherently spiritual nature of the Hawaiians, a way of thinking difficult to comprehend among westerners who adhere to the concept of private land ownership.

While the Big Island volcanoes call to mind the consuming nature of the elements, the rest of the Islands depict Hawai'i's nurturing, sustaining qualities. While Madame Pele consumes homes and builds new land apace—some three hundred new acres from the current eruption—families on all the islands are firing up their hibachis for sunset picnics on the beach. The smells of barbecues waft through the beach parks while in the uplands of Kōke'e, Kula, and Volcano, pungent wood smoke curls cheerfully from stone chimneys. Some urban professionals are still in their high-rise Honolulu offices, minutes away from becoming sunset joggers in the parks. In the ocean, there are surfers paddling toward the sinking sun, lured by the trough and crest of the waves that define their lives. Somewhere in Hawai'i at this moment, there is a lavish gathering in a hilltop mansion, a fisherman setting up his tarp shelter for the weekend, a cowboy scraping the mud from his boots. Somewhere in

Hawai'i at this moment, villagers are left homeless by a volcano's destruction while others exult in the benign beauty of this island environment.

Hawai'i's environment and climate have always been the key elements around which Islanders have tailored their lifestyles, living structures, and priorities. If there is such a thing as a Hawai'i style, it is the penchant

that Islanders have for inviting the outdoors indoors and the indoors outdoors. More than a specifically tropical ambience, it is this smooth, harmonious interplay between interior and exterior that is the signature of Hawai'i style. Foliage, flowers, breezes, colors, light—in the Island home they flow in and out unobtrusively, cheerfully blurring the boundaries between interior and exterior.

In the course of preparing this book, I encountered many who questioned the very existence of a distinct Hawai'i style, as if it were a single entity with a single definition, set in the context of a specific time. It would be impossible to examine Hawai'i in this way. These islands are diverse, with a Polynesian past and polyglot present, with a lifestyle defined by the environment, with a soul and dimension rooted in a profound love for the land. *Aloha 'āina*, as the Hawaiians call it, and a deep love of nature have defined the Hawaiian existence from the beginning. Today these values fight for survival amid the rampant development of modern-day Hawai'i, a land where lifestyle struggles to prevail over architecture, and legacies crumble daily in the rubble of forgotten buildings.

This is a book about the lifestyle and values that ideally define, and hopefully will outlive, the architecture of Hawai'i. It is not a book about architecture, nor is it a showcase for the preeminent designers of the time. The straightforward use of local materials, the indistinct boundaries between the indoors and outdoors, the informality and sense of place—these are the elements of Hawai'i style that leave the

conventional hierarchies of form and design to others in less gracious environments.

Some of the homes, such as plantation and *kama'āina* homes, have been classified in their physical or historical context, but others have been placed according to how they have been inhabited and styled. In these cases, where the design and construction of a house become secondary to what has been put in it, the definition of style hinges upon elements more notable than the house itself.

"Architects feel that architecture should express the values of its occupants and the community," notes Glenn Mason, a respected Honolulu architect who specializes in restoration work. "When you have the luxury to express lifestyles in every facet of a building design, when you can afford to, it's great. But that's become more and more difficult in recent years. As it becomes harder, you work more with the decorative elements rather than other aspects of the house."

The Hawaiians have always opened a new home with considerable ceremony and festivity. Even today, it's hard to find a new home

that has not been the recipient of a Hawaiian blessing or been opened with the traditional untying of a *maile* lei.

Consider this an untying of a *maile* lei, inviting all those present to enter the abodes of Islanders past and present. "*E komo mai,*" the Hawaiians would say. Welcome.

Hawai'i's journey into modern times began with rock and grass. Even today, majestic lava edifices and nineteenth-century wooden churches can be seen along deserted shorelines, country roads, even in the dense urban skyline of Honolulu. Silent echoes of the past, these structures persist in a world

eons away from their beginnings. From the start, when rock caves, or *hale pōhaku*, sheltered the earliest Hawaiians, Hawai'i's temperate conditions have spawned creative uses of natural materials. Houses made from the bark of *koa* trees, and then arched houses with wooden posts, followed the initial stone shelters. Soon the Hawaiian house had its sides and roof ingeniously thatched

with shiny, smooth *pili* grass, sugarcane leaves, *lauhala* (pandanus), banana bark, *koa* bark, coconut husk, ferns, *ti* leaves, and whatever else could be found. Once this house was completed, it embraced the outdoors once again: Woven *lauhala* sleeping mats and coarsely woven or plaited

Hawai'i THEN

sedge mats lined the floors, imbuing the interior with their earthy fragrances and textures.

Except for the *hale* without walls, such as the canoe house, the Hawaiian house had few, if any, windows, and they were small. To the Hawaiians, who were consummate outdoorsmen, the house was purely shelter—a place for sleeping, protected, after long, full days out of doors. There were houses of worship (*heiau*), separate houses for men and women to eat in, a house for sleeping, and common family dwellings for social gatherings. One type of house was made precisely

for beating *kapa*, the native bark cloth made of *wauke*, or paper mulberry, which women arduously transformed into soft, strong sheets for bedding and clothing. *Kapa* warmed the sleeping space in the center of the room, its folds embracing the outdoors and bringing its smells, fibers, and tactile delights into the interior environment.

If a house was constructed properly, according to the rules of building and choosing a site, reveals Hawaiian historian Samuel Kamakau in *The Works of the People of Old*, it was believed that the householder "would live to be white-haired, bent with age, dim-sighted; to crouch before the fire with wrinkled eyelids hanging down upon his cheeks or held up with sticks; to lie down feebly and be car-

ried about in a net; and to go away from the world of light as gently as the wafting of a zephyr."

The Hawaiians have always loved a good party, and a housewarming was no exception. At all levels of society, the warming of a house occasioned armloads of gifts and elaborate feasting, with family-style preparations that lasted several days. *Taro* was cooked vigorously and then pounded into *poi*, the sticky purple staple of the Hawaiians. Pits were dug in the earth, lined with hot lava rocks and leaves, and filled with chicken, dogs, pigs, yams, and breadfruit, which steamed and sizzled underground in the *imu* until the smoky unearthing several hours later. Finally, when the feast was ready and the owner had placed a ceremonial fish and *kapa* under the threshold of the front door, the house would be officially and prayerfully opened.

The historian Kamakau describes the ceremony as the cutting of the "navel cord" (*piko*) of the house. Just as a baby's umbilical cord is cut at birth, so did the Hawaiian house have its own birth ritual. A length of wood would be placed across the entrance to the house and a bunch of thatch laid over it. Then, explains Kamakau, "the owner of the house took hold of an adz and cut the bunch of thatch, the *piko*, praying meanwhile:

> *O Kāne, O Kū, O Lono,*
> *I am cutting the navel cord of*
> *the house, O gods,*
> *A house to revive life,*
> *A house to extend life . . .*

And so the prayer went, appealing for well-being for those who would make their lives there, and for all those who entered. The house, its navel cord cut, was born, and a new life begun.

Once the ceremony ended, great bunches of greenery were unfurled to cover and beautify the interior of the house. Everything from *palapalai* ferns to ginger and *maile*, an anise-scented leaf used as an offering to the ancient gods and goddesses, was generously distributed until the house was awash in nature's greens and drenched in their heady aromas. At last, after a final prayer, the feast was served, the gifts distributed, and the house officially and joyfully opened.

Grass House, Hawaii.

Pili grass and lava rock (above) were among the original building materials of the early Hawaiians, who used them to build sturdy thatched homes.

Opposite: A wall in Kapa'au, the Big Island, uses Hawai'i's oldest building material—lava rock, topped here with fishing balls.

Thatched structures (left) endure in Hawai'i, as in this pavilion in Miloli'i, one of the last traditionally Hawaiian villages.

Fronted by a green stalk of *ti*, whitewashed coral forms this wall (above) at the Mission Houses Museum, the Islands' first Christian mission. Coral was one of the natural building materials popular in the early nineteenth century.

A lava-rock wall in Kapa'au, Hawai'i island (above right). Coral block, cut from a nearby reef, appears in Kawaiaha'o Church (right). Similar coral structures can be found in Kailua-Kona's Hulihe'e Palace and Moku'aikaua Church.

The West Arrives

It's difficult to say when such elaborate housewarmings for such simple dwellings, and the spirit in which they were conducted, ceased to be the norm in Hawai'i. What is known is that the advent of western ways, beginning with the arrival of Captain James Cook in 1778, changed most things about the old Hawai'i. The sandalwood traders arrived in about 1810, the early whalers in 1819, and the first missionaries—who lived at first in grass houses—in 1820. Foreign trade, sugar plantations, and the immigrant labor they demanded lured waves of newcomers from east and west who would intermarry and make their homes here.

Some of these earliest influences can still be seen in Hawai'i. The Mission Houses Museum, erected in downtown Honolulu in 1821, is the oldest wooden house remaining in the Islands, a prominent throwback to the New England influence that followed the missionaries here. The museum is the only prefab wooden house remaining of the many that were brought from New England in the days before Hawai'i had its own fully functioning lumber mills.

Walls and pillars of lava rock, Hawai'i's oldest building material, still appear prominently in the humblest and grandest of homes. Some early lava-and-coral structures have endured, such as the Moku'aikaua Church and Hulihe'e Palace in Kailua-Kona, and downtown Honolulu's Kawaiaha'o Church, dedicated in 1842 as Honolulu's first church. There is also a schoolhouse on the grounds of Kawaiaha'o that was originally made with a thatched roof and adobe. Although the adobe walls are now hidden by plaster, the use of this material exemplified the westerners' search for masonry materials that would effectively replace thatch.

"People in Hawai'i used thatch until the turn of the century, but it became less and less common after 1850," explains architect Glenn Mason. "At first the missionaries used thatch because it was convenient. Almost all the early homes of westerners that weren't precut had

generous lānais and balconies. While the missionaries were used to living indoors in the harsh New England climate, here they began living outdoors." The arrival of the westerners also engendered what has become a common syndrome in Hawai'i: conflicting goals. "People in Hawai'i (a) want to be more like the mainland, and (b) want to be more uniquely Hawaiian," notes Mason. "It's push and pull, and at different times, we've emphasized one or the other."

The Kalāhikiola Church in Kapa'au, Hawai'i island (above), is typical of the wooden structures that followed the missionaries to Hawai'i.

A lava-rock church in Kīlauea, Kaua'i (above), and the Wai'oli Mission in nearby Hanalei (right) reflect the early missionary influences in Hawai'i. The flamboyant Queen Anne style of this Hilo missionary home (far right) shows off Victorian tastes in Hawai'i.

A simple home in Hawi, Hawai'i island (opposite), combines the missionary and plantation influences.

22

The Last King

It's no surprise that Hawai'i was looking to the west in the nineteenth century. King David Kalākaua, the "Merrie Monarch" and last king of Hawai'i, ascended to the throne in 1874 and immediately imbued his dynasty with the baroque, romantic grandeur he saw in the European monarchies of the time. He also resurrected the hula from a missionary-imposed disappearance and built 'Iolani Palace, the only royal palace on American soil. With his sister and successor, Queen Lili'uokalani, he entertained lavishly in its chandeliered and gilded rooms, among Corinthian columns, mirrored walls, and infinite panels of gleaming *koa* wood. 'Iolani Palace had the first flush toilets of any palace anywhere and the first electric-light and intra-house telephone systems in Hawai'i. In 1893, after American troops illegally overthrew the monarchy at 'Iolani Palace, it was renamed The Executive Building.

The coup of 1893 irrevocably planted the west (albeit by questionable means) in the political reality of these islands. Economically,

however, the ways of the west had taken hold decades earlier. Since the early 1800s, whaling, the sandalwood trade, ranching, and the sugar industry had sown the seeds of capitalism liberally in Hawai'i. Ever since the Reciprocity Treaty of 1876 allowed Hawaiian sugar duty-free entry to the United States, politics and influences in Hawai'i leaned discernibly more strongly to the *haole* (Caucasian) planter class.

The plantations, beginning with the 1835 opening of Kaua'i's Kōloa Plantation, were building a strong foundation in the Islands, and the immigrant labor they needed—Chinese, Japanese, Portuguese, Filipino—had been streaming in since the mid-1800s. Reflecting the increasingly hybrid nature of Hawai'i, homes in the Islands were built of local materials using western techniques. Coral, lava rock, adobe, 'ōhi'a logs, *koa* finishing, and imported materials such as Douglas fir were combined in new ways as Hawai'i searched for a style of its own. Beginning in the mid-1800s, explains Glenn Mason, the importation of California lumber caused a minor revolution in building.

"In a way, we developed before California did," he explains. "With the 1848 California gold rush, the Northwest and California opened up and all kinds of lumber mills were opened. We started to receive a lot of materials shipped from California, and building with those materials began to flourish in Hawai'i."

With the availability of lumber from the West Coast, the cross-cultural nature of Island construction fell out of favor. Stone, coral, and other heavy and hard-to-maneuver native materials became less popular than light, controllable wood. From 1890 to 1904, Hawai'i witnessed its first building boom.

"There was very much a conscious desire of the people here to emulate the U.S., to proclaim that we were westernized and could do it as well as the mainland could," continues Mason. "Many of the buildings that were built in that period, and up until 1920, emulate the United States."

Princess Ruth's ornate European-style house (left), built after 1907, is a contrast to the simplicity of traditional Hawaiian homes.

Opposite: Details of the exquisitely wrought Alexander and Baldwin building in downtown Honolulu, completed in 1929 and designed by the prominent architects C. W. Dickey and Hart Wood.

A Hawai'i Style

In the 1920s, a burgeoning group of architects, led by C. W. Dickey and Hart Wood, was moving to Hawai'i and making a mark on the Islands' building stock. Familiar with regional design movements on the mainland, they brought to Hawai'i a set of techniques in search of a local style. One avenue of exploration made abundant use of tile and stucco, popular in the sun-drenched Southwest and Mediterranean areas. Others explored combinations of stone and wood with steep, often double-pitched roofs which harkened back to the forms of ancient grass houses. Architects and builders were constantly searching for a statement that was singularly appropriate for Hawai'i.

Although those questions have never been settled, some characteristics unique to Hawai'i emerged from those discussions, and have endured. To this day, asserts Mason, Hawai'i style encompasses several definitive criteria, among them: a blurring between the interior and exterior of a house; *lānais* (porches), an Island signature; the use of natural ventilation, including high ceilings; and the use of local materials and design motifs.

As Hawai'i's increasingly diversified populace began to depart from the heavily western influences of the previous years, new decorative elements and motifs surfaced. They expressed, for the first time, the regional, multiethnic flavor of Hawai'i.

"There were local people saying, for the first time, 'We don't have to make it just like the mainland,'" asserts DeSoto Brown, an archivist at the Bernice Pauahi Bishop Museum in Honolulu. "The 1930s is when I think they began defining the decorative Hawaiian arts. The Oriental influences, as well as the Polynesian, attempted to deal realistically with the Hawaiian climate. This is when rattan got started in interiors. It was made in the Philippines, but this is where it got its start in the U.S."

Tropical nightclubs, such as Trader Vic's, also got their start in this period, and architects such as Roy C. Kelley, who was chief architect

The corrugated iron roof (top) crowns a colorful Buddhist temple in Hāmākua, a plantation town on Hawai'i island. The weathered stucco wall of a house on Diamond Head (above) reflects the Oriental influences that endure in Hawai'i.

The Ko'olau mountains on O'ahu cradle this Nu'uanu Valley home (left), its white stucco walls a dramatic canvas for its stylized, bonsai-like hedge.

The Bishop Museum facade (right), built in 1889, shows the use of gray lava stone quarried on the site. The architect C. W. Dickey's touches in the Hawaiian Telephone Co. building (far right) in Hilo, completed in 1931. Lava rock and painted concrete remain local signatures (below, left and right).

Opposite: Stone in many forms, from a wall on Maui (top left) to the remains of an old church in Hōnaunau, Hawai'i island (top right). Rock pillars and western trim in a Hilo home (center left) and weathered stucco in Makiki (center right). The historic C. Brewer building in Honolulu (bottom right) built in 1930. Note the prominent Dickey roofline and decorative elements popular in the thirties and forties.

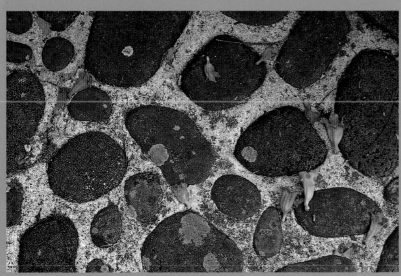

A tropical fish screen adorns a Nu'uanu, O'ahu, home (top). The Halekūlani Hotel in the 1950s (above), with *lauhala* mats, rattan, stained concrete floors, and bark-cloth curtains in exotic designs.

in Dickey's office, began designing apartments and homes in which rattan, *lānais*, and the high-pitched Hawaiian roofline, the Dickey trademark, proliferated. Decorative elements were distinctively Hawaiian, such as wooden panels, screens, and railings with cutout designs of anthuriums, breadfruit, monstera leaves, and the taro-like *'ape*. Swaying palm trees and exotic tropical flowers suddenly became silhouettes on curtains and etched glass. The highly stylized Mundorff flower prints and a streamlined Art Deco style popularized by the Matson liner menus of the thirties and forties became an Island trademark.

"It started out as highbrow but soon grew to become everybody's style," explains Brown of the new movement in Hawai'i. "It was so prevalent, you'd find it from Kalihi Valley on up. Gump's and Grossman Moody were the creators, I think, of this Hawaiian theme."

The two stores popularized the Hawaiian motifs in everything from silver platters to tropical leaf-shaped *koa* bowls, ivory necklaces, and Hawaiian charms. The *plumeria* and *pīkake* blossoms became ubiquitous as design images, appearing in everything from carved perfume bottles to scents purportedly derived from them. In addition, notes Brown, fabrics in these themes became popular upholstery coverings in the decades after the thirties, spreading romance to the mainland in yet another medium. It was, in the era of Waikīkī beachboys, luxury liners, and the "Hawaii Calls" radio program broadcast from Waikīkī Beach, a time of *hapa-haole* (half-Caucasian) music, ambience, and style. The other half was Hawaiian, and by the forties and fifties, when rattan, carved *koa*, and tropical motifs were ensconced in the Island home, there was, indeed, a Hawai'i style.

There are many, DeSoto Brown among them, who contend that Hawai'i style came and went as a definite era, disappearing with statehood in 1959 and the jet travel and high-rise boom of the 1960s. A certain sense of loss surrounds this premise. True, the colorful visual style that struggled to emerge in the twenties and thirties may have gone the way of dusty attics, auctions, and estate sales. And around every corner, bulldozers and foreign investment flex their muscles as they ravenously consume some of Hawai'i's most pleasing habitats.

What has outlived the transience of a visual style, though, and the era in which it is couched, is a style of living that somehow manages to endure and even flourish. Unmistakably contemporary, yet steeped in a sense of place, it has a patina all its own, an aesthetic independence that places certain elements above form and financial means. Hawai'i style is unendingly resourceful. Values and instincts coalesce to respond creatively to Hawai'i's climate and environment, celebrating modesty and grandeur in equal measure. Thus we have the surfer's beachside shack, the newly redeemed vagabond's house, the esteemed *kama'āina* estate, the modest plantation worker's home, the ramshackle mountain house, the avant-garde contemporary home—all equally marvelous, all equally Hawai'i style.

A home in Kapahulu, O'ahu (above left), is a study in nostalgia, with rattan, etched glass, and a *koa* table from the mid-twentieth century. The dining room (above) features some of the owner's collectibles, including a night-blooming cereus platter in the cabinet, probably from the original Gump's.

31

WELCOME TO
HAWAII ISLAND
HAWAII STATE
HAWAII COUNTY

"*In the Hawaiian mind, a sense of place was inseparably linked with self-identity and self-esteem. To have roots in a place meant to have roots in the soil of permanence and continuity.*"—George Kanahele, *Kū Kanaka*

Not many in Hawai'i can claim to have such roots. Here, where all but the Hawaiians are immigrants and expatriates, not many can claim to be *kama'āina*, a child of the land, or native-born. In a place of ever-increasing newcomers and ever-diminishing members of the Hawaiian host culture, *kama'āina* status has a cachet all its own. "We've lived on this land since before time was reckoned in the way we reckon it now," explains Hannah Kihalani Springer, whose great-great-great-great-grandparents are buried at the shoreline in Kakapa, Hawai'i island, not far from where she lives with her husband, Michael Tomich, and two children. "We've been landowners here since there were landowners here." **H**annah

can recount a lineage that goes back ninety-three generations, as far back as the *Kumuhonua*, a public record of genealogies and creation stories. Preserved in chants and as a written record, Springer's genealogy appears in a

Kama'āina

ledger passed down and written in a single hand. The writing stops at the generation of her great-great-grandparents. The genealogies, observes Springer, are "another sound Hawaiian tradition, a means of associating ourselves with our ancestors, their lifetimes and places."

Springer is *kama'āina* in its truest sense, with roots that reach as far back as you can go in Hawai'i, to the days before missionaries, a written language, even Kamehameha the Great—to the original Hawaiians who peopled the land. "Hawaiian history certainly began long before Kamehameha and the life and times the Euro-Americans were able to document," Springer asserts. Indeed, one of the earliest chants of the fire goddess Pele and her sister, Hi'iaka, mentions Hu'ehu'e, Hannah's ancestral homeland. Her daughter, Thelma Kihalani, is the fifth consecutive Kihalani on her mother's side. On Hannah's father's side, the lineage goes beyond Kame'eiamoku, a chief who appears on the coat of arms of the Kingdom of Hawai'i. Thelma Kihalani and her brother, Kekaulike Prosper, are the fourth generation of their family to live in their ninety-year-old home high on the slopes of Hualālai, one of the four great mountains of Hawai'i island.

The view from their front porch looks over the greened cinder cones and vast dryland forests of the Hu'ehu'e Ranch lands, once owned by Hannah's family. A dark, angular landmark nearby is Puhi-a-Pele, a spatter cone that pumped out voluminous quantities of fast-moving lava between December 1800 and January 1801, rearranging entire sections of the North Kona landscape. The terrain cascades gracefully to Kūki'o, a bay and beach known for its freshwater springs, where Hannah's ancestors played and fished for generations.

There is an irrevocable sense of continuity here, a love of place that has become increasingly rare in the fast-changing, fast-moving landscape of contemporary Hawai'i. Even the word *kama'āina* has come to mean different things with the passage of time. Today the word is loosely used as the opposite of *malihini*, or newcomer—someone familiar or acquainted with a place. Most commonly (and democratically), it means someone born in Hawai'i, whether of Asian immigrant background, or Portuguese, or any one of the gloriously golden mixtures that reflect the multiethnic flavor of Hawai'i.

Bottles and fishing balls from the region, generations-old native woods, and paintings by Pilipo Springer line the interior of Kukui'ohiwai: a red feather *kahili* and a portrait of the owner's great-great-grandmother (above and above right), priceless *kou* bowls and a *koa*-lidded coconut hatbox from four generations ago (right), and, in the corner, Pilipo Springer paintings (far right).

Opposite: Kukui'ohiwai (top), once a ranch house, still presides over the ancestral homelands. The front porch (bottom) of one of the twelve buildings on the property.

Names and Places

To be a worthy proponent of *kama'āina* style, however, one must embrace place, tradition, and nature in a way that no other style approaches. One must live up to the word. A *kama'āina* in Hawai'i resides in a place in which 86 percent of the place names are in the Hawaiian language. Many *kama'āina* homes are immortalized in Hawaiian songs, just as every surf break offshore, even if just twenty yards from the next, enjoys its own moniker.

"How many place names are there or were there in the Hawaiian Islands?" muses Samuel H. Elbert in his introduction to the book *Place Names of Hawaii*, which he wrote with Mary Kawena Pukui and Esther T. Mookini. "Even a rough estimate is impossible: a hundred thousand? a million? Hawaiians named taro patches, rocks and trees that represented deities and ancestors, sites of houses and *heiau* (places of worship), canoe landings, fishing stations in the sea, resting places in the forests, and the tiniest spots where miraculous or interesting events are believed to have taken place."

The *kama'āina* tradition in Hawai'i shares similarities with Australia's Aborigines, who for centuries have traveled the invisible pathways of the Outback bringing places, animals, and everything they encounter into existence through the power of song. Even today, the Hawaiian oral tradition immortalizes special places through chants and music. *"Na Kulaīwi Kaulana,"* meaning "those famous homes," is a concert (and a recording) that traveled throughout Hawai'i paying

This prominent and distinctive manse (left, top to bottom) on O'ahu is called Papakōlea Moanalua, or "the plover flats of Moanalua Valley." It was hewn from hand-carved bluestone. The different parts of the house were built and connected in 1900, 1928, and 1941.

tribute to the distinguished families and homes of Hawai'i. Everything from coconut groves to artesian pools to rambling plantation homes and palatial *kama'āina* estates, many of them long gone, is recalled poetically and with great affection.

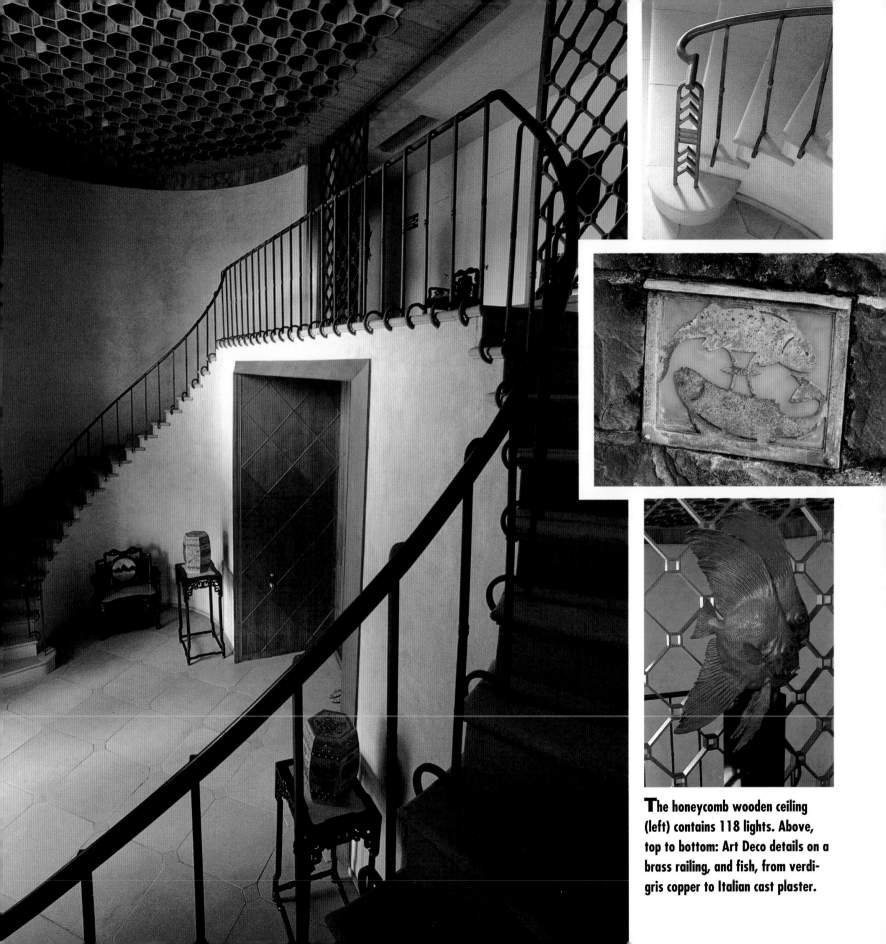

The honeycomb wooden ceiling (left) contains 118 lights. Above, top to bottom: Art Deco details on a brass railing, and fish, from verdigris copper to Italian cast plaster.

The living room's sliding doors of brass and glass (above) open up to views of Salt Lake, O'ahu. A single piece of finely woven *lauhala* lines the ceiling in a living room of Australian willow (above right).

An heirloom mahogany four-poster, curly *koa* tables, and Australian willow walls (right) add warmth to the master bedroom.

Gilded Austrian crystal wineglasses (top) have been handed down in the family. Australian willow adds a burnished glow to this living room corner (above), where fishing lures and a lamp trimmed with coconut fiber reflect an Island lifestyle.

Fishing balls found by the owner's father, a *koa* calabash, and a painting of the owner's great-great-grandmother express a sense of place and history (left).

◆◆◆◆◆◆◆◆◆◆◆◆◆◆◆◆◆◆◆◆◆◆

Singing Hawai'i

Although most of these songs were written and are sung in Hawaiian, even listeners who don't know the language are enveloped in their intimacy and grace. There is humor, a profound love for the land, and vignettes encompassing legend, mythology, history, botany, and the simple exaltation of mountains, sea, and surroundings. "Life is peaceful in the cool shade of the *kiawe*, in the gentle swaying of the coconut leaves, in calm whispering waters at the seashore," wrote the late Helen Desha Beamer, in Hawaiian, about Keawa'iki, the Big Island retreat of noted *kama'āina* Francis I'i Brown. "Bathe in the fresh spring in the lava, crystal clear and cold, body tingling when rising out of the water, body tingling when rising out of the water . . ."

"We used to go there as children," recalled the late Charles K. L.

Davis, one of Hawai'i's great voices, who assembled the songs and hosted the program with singer Nalani Olds. "To get to Keawa'iki, we'd get on a boat at Kawaihae or we'd be sent behind the Kona nightingales [mules] with the commodities. I used to put on my brand-new tennis shoes and hike over the *'a'a* [crumbly lava], and by the time we got there, half the soles of my shoes were gone."

Davis remembered the chanters who always accompanied a Hawaiian retinue. "There was a person of note who would precede the chanter, and the chanter would follow, singing the ancestry of the family and the name of the person and the details of the genealogy," he recalled. "In so many places that the Hawaiians had, there was a certain feeling—a feeling that there was something special about the place. It would come over anyone who went there. It could be a sudden stillness, a wonderful rapport."

Helen Desha Beamer immortalized this quality in the rich legacy of music she left behind. "Paniau" describes the four mountains of

Hawai'i—Mauna Kea, Mauna Loa, Hualālai, the Kohala Mountains—plus Maui's Haleakalā, visible from the west shore of the Big Island where this *kama'āina* home is located. The views of the mountains from the freshwater lava pool, and descriptions of the types of foliage surrounding it, establish a sense of place uniquely Hawaiian. Often this affection outlives the place itself, as it has in "Puamana," written by Irmgard Farden Aluli of her family home on Maui. Once ringing with the laughter of twelve children, Puamana has long been sold, its house replaced by another, but its yard still bordered by the twelve coconut trees planted decades ago by the Farden children.

Indeed, *kama'āina* style has the ability to bridge time, place, and people with grace and wit. "There is a *kama'āina* style of speaking, a *kama'āina* style of dressing, a *kama'āina* style of doing things," explains songwriter Irmgard Farden Aluli. "But if you're talking about a way of living, it means following the ways of the native, of what is dictated as Hawaiian. *Kama'āina* style means Hawaiian hospitality."

This Kohala Coast family beach home is an oasis sprouting out of arid lava. Large carp swim in fish ponds, and boats are at the ready a few feet from the ocean.

The Open Door

No one is expected today to invite strangers in to dine, as the old Hawaiians used to do, but there are many elements in a *kama'āina* home that revolve around social exchange. "We always think of openness as Hawaiian style," continues Aluli. "We like to have porches, be open to nature, enjoy the yard. And there's a casualness about it, a quality that's inviting. I have a big *pūne'e* [movable couch]. The first thing you think is, 'I can relax and stretch out on that.' If you had formal upright chairs, they wouldn't lend themselves to easy living."

The Hawaiians taught the missionaries a thing or two about easy living. As the missionaries moved into the political and power structure of these islands, and as they intermarried with the Hawaiians, they, too, became *kama'āina*. Today many of Hawai'i's finest *kama'āina* homes are those built by prominent missionary families in the days before Hawai'i had navigable roads and its own lumber mills.

On the north shore of Kaua'i, a historic home called Kauikeōlani is a testament to the grand style of the early missionaries. Built in the 1890s from logs floated into Hanalei Bay, this sprawling landmark tells the story of A. S. Wilcox, the son of Abner and Lucy, Hanalei's most prominent missionaries. A.S. was the entrepreneur nonpareil who planted three thousand coconut trees on the property and sold the meat to the Chinese in Honolulu, who eagerly bought it for their candy. Wilcox also leased land to rice and taro farmers and boldly attempted to establish his own plantation with crops in coffee, sugar, cotton, and silk. To supply himself and friends with firewood for their stoves, he planted groves of ironwood trees that green the area today. He also raised cattle, and, when he married a Hawaiian woman named Kauikeōlani, he named his home after her.

"Kauikeōlani was noted for her hospitality," explains Patsy

Nostalgia and tranquillity prevail at this fifteen-acre lava-rock beach estate (opposite and left). Fishing balls and stone poi pounders from the area, hula dolls, and trophies are among the family's collectibles.

Opposite: The veranda of Kauikeōlani (left) wraps around three-quarters of the building. The stately *kama'āina* home in Hanalei, Kaua'i (top right), has a boathouse overlooking one of two fishponds on the property (center right), seven bedrooms, five bathrooms, and four different entrances to the living room (bottom right).

Sheehan, A. S. Wilcox's great-granddaughter, who now owns Kauikeōlani. "She was known for her great *poi* suppers. When Prince Kūhiō came to Hanalei, they hosted him with banners and a big party. He came in by boat and they rowed him in, and we have pictures of them standing on the steps, with bunting on the house. The house was used very much that way, in that time."

As a child, Sheehan climbed the tall, spindly coconut trees to gather their unwieldy fruit. She recalls picking ferns for the tables at their large family suppers while others dispersed to pick *'opihi* (limpets, a Hawaiian delicacy) and gather crabs from traps they had set in the bay across the road. There were chickens and pigs in the backyard, ducks roaming the yard, and an *imu* (underground rock oven) that was fired up regularly. The garden provided tomatoes, rhubarb, lettuce, and greens, and even today, oranges and grapefruit dangle bountifully in the yard.

When guests arrived, recalls Sheehan, all social activity moved from the informal breakfast room to the spacious living and dining rooms. "The living room has four entrances and exits, and the porch goes around three-quarters of it," explains Sheehan. "It's a big rectangle, and you can get at it from all sides. One side is close to the kitchen, the other end looks at Hanalei Bay. And because it's six to seven feet off the ground, there's enough height to see the water."

"This is Hawaiian style," adds noted Honolulu architect Spencer Leineweber. "At one end of the social spectrum, you may be drinking beer and eating *poke* [seasoned raw fish] in the garage. This is the other end of that spectrum. The social pattern, the organization of space, is the same. It's very Hawaiian. It's a shared community space."

An arbored pathway in Hā'ena, East Hawai'i Island, traverses the land where *nene* thrive.

Opposite: A ten-acre estate in Olinda includes two gabled homes, one (top) built in 1902. The garden is decorated with urns (bottom left) made by a relative of the owner in the late nineteenth century. The view from the pool of the newer house (bottom right) looks over the West Maui mountains.

The newer home of the Olinda estate, designed by C. W. Dickey and built in 1912 with eleven gables, was recently renovated but retains some features of the original building. A bathroom (above left) and stairway (above right) combine old and new elements. The pre-1900 Regina music box at the foot of the stairs (right) still works, and the 1936 Caphart record player and radio continues to play 78's. A buffet of curly *koa* (far right) is carved with *plumeria* blossoms and mangoes. The *koa* and Monterey pine bowls were turned by the owner.

Curbing the Hula

There was, however, a less-than-democratic cultural hierarchy imposed by the missionaries and supported by Ka'ahumanu, Kamehameha the Great's queen regent and the most prominent convert to Christianity. Appalled by the ribald behavior of the whalers who were streaming to Hawai'i's harbors, the missionaries banned Hawaiian women from their ships and wasted no time in attempting to abolish the hula. They clothed the Hawaiians in high-necked, puritanical garb and put the fear of God in them, changing forever the carefree, spirited, Polynesian nature of the people.

Even today, there are those who associate *kama'āina* style with the repressive *haole* (Caucasian) practices of the early missionaries. Although rooted in the Hawaiian way, *kama'āina* came to be associated with elitism, applied either to Hawaiian nobility or to the *haole* missionaries. As Patsy Sheehan points out, attitudes differed even then.

"A. S. Wilcox spoke fluent Hawaiian, and he lived with Hawaiians, and his mother and father taught Hawaiians," she explains. "In Hanalei Valley, they had a closer relationship with the Hawaiians than most. It was not something A.S. dealt with on a different class level."

Once they made the transition from the constricted, indoor, New England lifestyle to the sensuous informality of the tropics, the missionaries were unstoppable. Oceanfront living suited them, as did the rigors of the ranching or plantation life that often succeeded a life with the church. Hā'ena, a seventeen-thousand-acre Big Island estate, was built by missionaries as a cattle ranch, and is today the home of Jackie and Roy Shipman Blackshear and their flock of *nene*, the indigenous Hawaiian geese snatched from extinction by Roy's uncle, Herbert Shipman.

Sprawling Kīkīla in Lā'ie Malo'o (right, above and below), the second home in Hawai'i built with the C. W. Dickey roof, sits on an artesian well that is still in use. Opposite: a large veranda and a family room (top, center and right) bespeak a house of recreation. *Lauhala* mats and a Hawaiian quilt (bottom, center and right) are legacies from a rich past.

◆◆◆◆◆◆◆◆◆◆◆◆◆◆◆◆◆◆◆◆◆◆◆◆

The Geese Survive

Immortalized in an oil painting in the Blackshears' living room are Emma and Ka'iulani, the two female *nene* who produced ninety-five offspring and eventually reestablished the *nene* population in the Islands. The descendant of Boston missionaries, Herbert Shipman (who also introduced the orchid to Hawai'i) lost all but twelve of his flock in the 1946 tsunami that decimated much of east Hawai'i. With typical missionary grit, and the help of English ornithologists, he not only saved his flock, he regenerated the entire species.

Today Hā'ena is a *nene* sanctuary with a four-acre freshwater pond they roam and feed on freely, only a few feet from the ocean. Hā'ena is also where Hopoe, a poet and friend of Hi'iaka, the loyal sister of the

volcano goddess Pele, is said to have performed the first hula in the days when goddesses walked among mortals.

"There was a rock in the waters offshore that was called Ka Wahine Ho'olewa I Ke Kai—the undulating woman of the sea," recalls Charles K. L. Davis. "Roy used to row me out to the spot, and when the water was crystal clear and the light just right, you could see what looked like a woman with long black hair and a hula skirt, undulating with the tide. She looked like she was dancing the hula, and she was supposed to be the goddess Hopoe. It was the dancing rock of Hopoe." Although the 1946 tsunami dislocated the rock, it failed to topple the myth or the memory. "Lei O Hā'ena," another of Helen Desha Beamer's songs, recalls Hopoe, the lovely maiden of Hā'ena, as she danced among the "beautiful feathered birds" in the *hala* groves of Kea'au.

Within the Blackshear home, mountains of memorabilia recall the past: nineteenth-century paintings of Big Island scenes; carved turtle collections; an invitation to King David Kalākaua's coronation, at which he crowned himself; and a prescription for digitalis written by Kalākaua in 1890. There is sheet music from Queen Lili'uokalani, the king's sister, and one of the first *koa* wood dressers made in Hawai'i, built in 1850. A four-poster bed of *kauila*, a rare and dense hardwood used in Hawaiian weaponry, occupies the guest room just beyond the foyer where Herbert Shipman was found to have stored his bootlegged *'ōkolehao*. Recent renovations unearthed a fake ceiling wherein Uncle Herbert had stashed his potent Hawaiian liquor since 1937. As for the imposing *kauila* bed, it broke a lathe and repelled all nails before finally being dispatched to the ironworks, where it took a high-powered steel lathe to finish the job.

In the living room, a large Buddhist temple bell looks vaguely out of place amid the plethora of Hawaiian artifacts. Built in Japan more than a century ago, it was only recently carted, in a wheelbarrow and with great ceremony, across the lawn and into the ninety-year-old missionary home. It was a gift, a thank you, from the local Buddhist community. In typically Hawaiian fashion, the Blackshears had given them the plot of land on which their church stands, so that they, too, could have roots in Hawaiian soil.

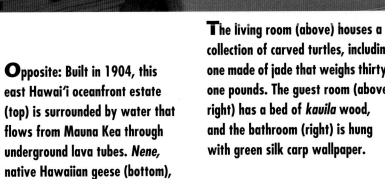

Opposite: Built in 1904, this east Hawai'i oceanfront estate (top) is surrounded by water that flows from Mauna Kea through underground lava tubes. *Nene,* native Hawaiian geese (bottom), feed in the large freshwater pond.

The living room (above) houses a collection of carved turtles, including one made of jade that weighs thirty-one pounds. The guest room (above right) has a bed of *kauila* wood, and the bathroom (right) is hung with green silk carp wallpaper.

Noted architect C. B. Ripley designed this 1920 one-and-a-half-story home in Nu'uanu, O'ahu. The shaded *lānai* (above) is made for entertaining, as is the dining room (left).

Opposite: Biedermeier furniture in the balcony-lined living room (top and bottom left). Historical photographs and a Hawaiian quilt in the guest bedroom (bottom right) combine European elegance with Hawaiian style.

At one time the most troublesome area of plantation life, plantation houses have outlived their creators to become one of Hawai'i's most enduring styles. The plantation home succeeds anywhere in Hawai'i. Ubiquitous, adaptable, and striking in its simplicity, it is the epitome of Hawai'i style. **N**otes Honolulu architect Spencer Leineweber, "If you look at its different elements, you'll find parts that are uniquely Hawaiian: the veranda, the steeply pitched roof that keeps air moving and rain off, the aesthetic based on simplicity. The materials are quite light. The plantation home has basically an inch of material between the inside and the outside. Unlike in the Caribbean, you rarely find thick walls here." **A**lthough dwarfed by the sprawling subdivisions of contemporary Hawai'i, tiny

wooden workers' homes still dot the countryside, a throwback to when life was governed by the whistle and "King Cane" ruled the Islands. In those days, workers' homes were built as cheaply as possible, while those of owners and managers reflected the genteel lifestyle of the plantation society.

Plantation

Taro, Sugar, and Pineapple

It has been a century and a half since the sugar and pineapple plantations established themselves in Hawai'i, and even longer since Kamehameha the Great, who unified the Hawaiian Islands, developed his *taro* plantation in O'ahu's Nu'uanu Valley. Proud indeed of the neat patches of *taro* that grew far up into the valley, it was he who was Hawai'i's first plantation boss. It is said that Kamehameha constructed his farmhouses high on a hill in Nu'uanu, allowing him panoramic views of his plantation kingdom as he gazed up and down the valley to the sea.

No doubt the *haole* bosses of the sugar and pineapple plantations took a similar kind of pride in surveying the undulating fields of green. They imported labor and built an industry, adapting, in fits and spurts, to the mechanization that came inevitably. And they had help along the way. The Reciprocity Treaty of 1876, the diplomatic coup of King David Kalākaua, removed the tariff on Hawaiian sugar and gave Hawai'i's plantations an enormous advantage in the marketplace. One year before the treaty, Hawai'i had twenty plantations; four years after the treaty, there were sixty-three. Although the situation in trade and politics continued to fluctuate through the years, Hawai'i experienced an agriculturally based boom that was unstoppable from the 1890s into the early twentieth century.

Today a $329 million industry, sugar is still the top agricultural crop in Hawai'i, followed by the $216 million pineapple industry. The economic and social power they once wielded in the Islands has long waned, however: Only thirteen sugar plantations employ fifty-four hundred workers today, a far cry from the early 1950s, when one in every seven Hawai'i residents, or about 14 percent, lived in sugar plantation communities.

Colorful wooden plantation-style homes with corrugated metal roofs dot Hawai'i's countryside. Top to bottom: Hāmākua coast, Hawai'i; Lā'ie, O'ahu; Holualoa, Hawai'i.

"You'd never see anything fancy in the workers' homes," explains Mike Faye of the Kīkīaola Land Co., which owns the Waimea Plantation Cottages, an ambitious restoration project in west Kauaʻi. "Architecturally, they had board and batten, a tin roof, X-bracing, and sash windows. They were built cheaply, because the sugar companies wanted to minimally comply with their contractual obligations."

Plantation managers' homes were often quite luxurious. This manager's house (right) in Kukuihaele, the Big Island, is still a majestic edifice, although it is currently unoccupied.

Those obligations included housing, medical care, and living expenses for the contract workers who were imported to work on the plantations. Following a short-lived attempt to wrest native Hawaiians from the *taro* farming and fishing they enjoyed, the plantations imported Chinese laborers by the droves, under contracts negotiated by the governments. The first contract laborers arrived from China in 1852, two years after the government of Hawaiʻi enacted a law allowing foreigners to own fee simple (legally owned) land.

The sugar growers were the first to stand in line for the low-priced acreage offered by Hawaiian chiefs and commoners, ingenues in real estate who had had their first taste of land ownership only when the Great Māhele of 1848 redistributed lands previously owned by the king. By 1890, 75 percent of Hawaiʻi's privately owned land was held by *haoles* or their companies. In later years, Hawaiʻi's prominent Big Five corporate oligarchy—American Factors, C. Brewer, Alexander and Baldwin, Castle and Cooke, and T. H. Davies—expanded its dominance in sugar production into retail, transportation, banking, tourism, and every other arena of commerce and power in the Hawaiian Islands.

Some of the Big Five families had their homes designed by prominent architects such as Charles William Dickey, related to a Big Five family, and his partner, Hart Wood. Steep-pitched rooflines, large *lānais*, and the use of stucco, lava, or natural materials characterized the gracious, patrician homes they designed for the wealthy. Dickey also left his mark on the Alexander and Baldwin building, the most memorable in downtown Honolulu.

The Waimea Plantation Cottages on Kaua'i are being bought from the nearby sugar company, moved to the oceanside, and restored.

Opposite: The twenty-acre Kīlauea manager's home on Kaua'i is the only one in Hawai'i made of stockpiled field rock.

The Manager's House

It was not Dickey, however, or any of his well-known cohorts who designed what is today one of the most stunning homes in Hawai'i. It was L. David Larsen, the manager of the Kīlauea Sugar Co., who created Hawai'i's only stone house for a plantation manager. With a triangular office, floors, bookcases, and doors of 'ōhi'a wood, with hinges and hardware made by a California blacksmith, the home remains a paragon of gracious living. Refurbished extensively by its present owners, it presides over a twenty-acre idyll of ponds, banyans, bamboo, and lava-rock terraces and pathways, its sweeping, stone-pillared verandas seamlessly blending the indoors and outdoors.

"When it came to the plantation manager's houses, they were more like country estates," asserts Mike Faye of Kīkīaola Land Co. "All in all, the identifying element was that most things were homemade. By and large, they used indigenous materials. They didn't, for example, bring in marble from Italy."

The Kōloa Plantation on Kaua'i was the first to open its doors in 1835. Founder William Hooper of Boston hired twenty-five Hawaiians at two dollars each per month, giving them small plots of land on which to grow food and a barrel of fish every three weeks. They shopped in the plantation store, lived in their own thatched homes, and eventually witnessed the departure of their employer. Disgusted by the hardships of rheumatism, isolation, and what he saw as the devious ways of native workers, Hooper left Hawai'i within four years.

Chinese laborers were brought in to augment and eventually replace the Hawaiians, whose numbers were dwindling because of introduced diseases—from a population of over 800,000 at the time Captain Cook arrived, to fewer than 50,000 at the time of reciprocity a century later. As the demand for labor accelerated, the Japanese were brought in to shore up the work force, followed by the Portuguese, Norwegians, Germans, Russians, Spaniards, and Filipinos.

A *plumeria* tree (above left) and large gracious pools (left) enhance the yard. The wide veranda (above and right) blends the indoors and outdoors. The house, which took two years to build and originally cost $18,000, was an experiment later declared a smashing success.

Opposite: On the grounds of the sixty-four-year-old Kīlauea plantation manager's home, a sweeping "flight" of steps were cut into the earth in a bamboo grove.

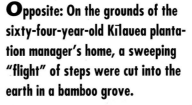

61

Inside the plantation manager's home, the entryway (above) is enhanced by a finely woven *lau-hala* rug made in Tonga.

Exotic artifacts from the Sepik River region of Papua New Guinea, and stalks of lobster claw heliconia from the garden enliven the washhouse (above right).

On this twenty-acre estate, the day begins in the breakfast nook (right), where a colorful array of treasured collectibles reigns.

Bookcases and floors of 'ōhi'a wood, a nineteenth-century Japanese screen, and a collection of calabashes made of rare *kou* wood enhance the living room (left).

This light, airy kitchen (below left) was made for entertaining.

The uneven contours of uncut rock can be seen beneath the concrete in the dining room walls of this manager's home in Kīlauea (below). Visible are three works from the owner's collection of Diamond Head paintings: one by Theodore Wores on the left, one by the owner's great-grandmother in the upper right, and beneath it, D. Howard Hitchcock's view of the landmark.

The Old Worker's House

Adding to the already harsh life in the fields and mills were the workers' living conditions. They started out as barbarous. "Housing continued for many years to be a focus of trouble for many of Hawai'i's plantations," writes Ed Beechert in *Working in Hawaii, a Labor History*. "Housing continued to be haphazard for many years; in fact, housing remained a matter of chance until labor acquired the power to strike." Even then, adds Beechert, rumblings of dissatisfaction about plantation housing were reported as late as 1966.

"We didn't have an indoor bathroom until I was in the fourth grade," recalls Robert "Puggy" Pagdilao, born in 1945 and raised in O'ahu's 'Ewa Plantation, considered a model plantation community. "I didn't wear shoes until the seventh grade. There were four children in our family. We first lived in a two-bedroom house that was built in the twenties, but my father added to the house as we got older. Then he got promoted, and on the plantation, the promotion got you a new house."

Pagdilao says he never realized they were poor until after high school. "It didn't seem as if anybody needed anything on the plantation," he observes pleasantly. "I had a very happy life. I never knew we were poor because everybody I knew was poor." By the time his father retired at age seventy, he had purchased the property for $23,000 and the house for a dollar. After working for the plantation from sixteen to sixty-five years old, he was able to benefit from management's prevailing practice of moving housing responsibilities to employees through below-market sales.

Most plantation workers in the senior Pagdilao's generation, and earlier, lived in racially segregated camps, with barracks-type dwellings for single men. A barracks could house anywhere from six to forty men, with kitchen facilities, when they had them, in a separate structure.

Nothing more than shelter and a place of rest was attempted, and privacy was nonexistent. When the plantations began importing families, crude partitions converted a barracks to a family room.

"Generally, they had a series of outbuildings," explains Mike Faye. "There was a *furo* [Japanese bath] house, a storage area, an old cook house, kitchen, and a bathhouse that was often just a tool shack. Because the houses were small and utilitarian, there wasn't a lot of extra space."

Informal gambling, alcohol, and the use of opium among the Chinese added to the complications of the marginal living conditions. In some camps, the "kitchen" consisted of a wood fire hastily erected in the dirt, and a couple's quarters could be six feet square.

Conditions improved with time, most dramatically after 1919, when the Hawaiian Sugar Planters Association, in response to labor strife and vociferous and violent protest, developed a new set of standardized blueprints for its workers' homes. Some plantation authorities go as far as to speculate that the new blueprints, and the newfound privacy they provided, helped fuel a baby boom that, years later, significantly affected the outcome of World War II.

"Before 1919, there were several families living in one house," observes one plantation official. "In 1920, many babies were born, with the Japanese the predominant minority. When World War II broke out, here were all these AJAs [Americans of Japanese ancestry] coming out to serve their country." Many of the soldiers in the 100th Battalion and the 442nd Regimental Combat Team, the much-decorated volunteer nisei combat groups that made significant gains in the war, were the offspring of plantation immigrants.

Opposite: A hundred-year-old Chinese rice planter's house in Hanalei, Kaua'i, is now the home of an artist.

The former planter's home is filled with works by the artist resident: shell leis and a turn-of-the-century Chinese silk robe (right); eggs made of sea glass and shells from local beaches (below left); shell-and-glass "Fat Ladies" (below center); a mirror wreathed in glass, shells, and broken-off gallon-jar loops from the Kaua'i shores (below right).

The New Worker's House

According to HSPA records, the plantations spent more than $3 million on revamping their housing between 1922 and 1925. Five years later, in 1930, another set of blueprints was unveiled. These massive programs of remodeling, repair, and construction, called "rehabilitation" by plantation authorities, brought sorely needed sanitation and comfort to the beleaguered plantation communities.

"While many splendid improvements have been accomplished, there is much to be done before all of our plantation villages can meet present-day standards," noted the *Hawaiian Planters' Record* of January 1926. "We recognize that contentment with the housing and surroundings certainly has its effect on man's producing power. . . ."

In this paternalistic, hierarchical society, the houses for skilled and semiskilled laborers differed, as did homes for workers (utilitarian), overseers (comfortable), and managers (luxurious). Of course, it was the *haole* owners and managers who presided over the plantation hierarchy, followed by the overseers, called *luna*, who were predominantly Portuguese, Hawaiian, and *haole*. The ethnically mixed mechanics, carpenters, and tradespeople fell under them in a kind of middle ground, while at the bottom of the scheme came the laborers who toiled in the fields and mills. "The fairer your skin was, somehow that would be worked into a bigger house," comments Faye wryly.

According to Beechert, a report by a Philippines labor investigator to the Philippine government in 1919 summarized the housing situation this way: "The Filipinos were generally housed in old structures inferior to the dwellings of laborers of other nationalities, especially to those of the Portuguese . . . and of the Japanese, who have fairly comfortable and well-conditioned dwellings."

The Dickey roofline appears on a worker-style home in Hilo, Hawai'i (left). Opposite: A corrugated roof tops a house in South Kona.

Even as late as the l950s, when Puggy Pagdilao was growing up, the racial lines on the plantations seemed inviolable. "There was a *haole* club where we couldn't go, and we couldn't date Japanese girls," says Pagdilao, who is Filipino. "The only girls we could date were Portuguese or Hawaiian. Everybody knew the rules and you wouldn't step on anybody's toes. Even through all this prejudice, though, the families were close. We learned from each other."

Pagdilao recalls his 'Ewa neighborhood: "Tenney Village was mixed, with Portuguese and Japanese. Then there was Banana Camp, with only Filipinos. C village was for Filipinos and Japanese, and that's where the Japanese school used to be. Filipino Camp later became Fernandez Village, where my parents live now. There was another camp called Lower Village, even though it was high on a hill. That was for the Japanese and Filipinos." Pagdilao's camp, called Middle Village, was a small complex of thirty homes in the middle of the cane fields, at the end of a washboard dirt road they called "Holey Road."

According to Mike Faye, the camps had come to be fairly integrated by the time the 1930s rolled around. "The plantations were not segregating them in a negative sense," he claims, "but so the different ethnic groups could continue their ethnic traditions."

Those traditions included Christmas-tree decorating for the Germans, who introduced the custom (along with potato salad) to plantation life. New Year's meant *mochi*-pounding for the Japanese, who also donned their kimonos and blue-and-white headbands to drum and dance their way through the O-bon dance season every summer. The *sake*, or rice wine, of their homeland steeped secretly in hidden bathtubs, its distinctive aroma wafting through the neighborhood like a blatant olfactory signal. They practiced *kendo*, *aikido*, and other martial arts and taught them to kids from other neighborhoods. For the Filipinos, the big cultural event was December 30, Rizal Day, when they honored their revolutionary leader, José Rizal.

Every Chinese New Year's, the Chinese lit long chains of noisy firecrackers and festooned their homes with colorful flags. Throughout the year, the Portuguese made spicy sausages and baked bread in traditional outdoor brick ovens that imbued the neighborhood with

pleasing aromas. The Hawaiians would dry their fish and *kalua* their pigs and dogs in underground rock ovens while the camps resonated with music from the different instruments introduced by the laborers. The Hawaiians and Portuguese had their *ukulele*, the Japanese and Okinawans their *samisen* and *shakuhachi*, the Filipinos their mandolins and guitars.

◆◆◆◆◆◆◆◆◆◆◆◆◆◆◆◆◆◆◆◆◆◆◆◆◆◆

Growing Up on the Plantation

Leisure was as pleasant as the field work was harsh. Gardens, each with its own character, flourished. "The single men had community gardens," recalls Pagdilao. "With school out at three, we used to go and pick pumpkin and squash from their gardens to bring home. The Japanese had Hayden mangos, lichees, *won bok* [Chinese cabbage], green onions, and rock gardens in front. You could tell the Filipino houses because they had lima beans or long green beans growing on the fence, with their victory gardens in the front of the house."

Team sports engaged the kids in intra-camp competition. "That's how you got known on a plantation, through sports," explains Pagdilao. "We'd always whip the Japanese at basketball and football, and they'd win at baseball." When the sugarcane was high, the children played chase master and hide-and-seek, losing themselves in the maze of tall, swaying green stalks that surrounded them on all sides.

"We didn't have toys, so we played outdoors," continues Pagdilao. "We played with paper milk covers, we played hopscotch and jump rope. And the plantation workers made homemade tops for us."

He also remembers filling the three-foot-deep, ten-by-ten-foot community *furo* with water and using it as a swimming pool. When the nights were cool, the children stoked the fire to heat the *furo* before the workers came home. "We went hiking, bike riding, sliding down the side of a hill. And because 'Ewa Beach was three miles away and I had no transportation, I learned to swim in the flumes."

Plantation children learned to swim in reservoirs and flumes. Middle Village, where Pagdilao grew up, was divided into north and south sections by the flume that traversed the camp. It originated about three hundred yards up the hill, near the plantation hospital.

"The water was pure, from an artesian well. It was cold and clean. We'd jump in at the hospital and ride the flume down to our camp," recounts Pagdilao. "It was covered with big, thick wire meshes until it got to our camp. It was about four feet deep, and when the water got rough toward the bottom, we'd grab the wooden bars across the flumes to slow down, and our friends would reach in to help."

The ravenous children would then head for the village bakery, which sold eclairs at five for a quarter. A small cup of saimin, a Hawaiian noodle soup, went like hotcakes for a nickel; and ten cents would get you a medium. Barbecued meat sticks, called teriyaki, a favorite local accompaniment for saimin, sold for ten cents in Pagdilao's day.

About two doors down from their home was the camp's center of cockfighting, a favorite pastime of the Filipinos and a tradition that continues today. "My father did surgery on the winning chickens. He was good at fixing their wounds," Pagdilao recalls. "I would hold the chicken while he repaired it. 'Remember this chicken?' he'd say. 'This is a three-time winner.'" After being fined for fighting cocks on his daughter's graduation day, the senior Pagdilao never indulged again.

Their workdays were punctuated by the whistle that defined the rhythm of the day. Even today on Lāna'i, an island privately owned by Castle and Cooke for its rapidly shrinking pineapple production and a new tourism venture, the plantation whistle still pierces the air like clockwork in the predawn hours or at eight o'clock for curfew.

"We lived by the whistle," Pagdilao remembers. "It used to blow every weekday at five-thirty to wake up the men, and at seven to start work. It would sound again for lunch, and you could hear it from one side of 'Ewa to the other. After lunch it would blow again, and at three, when they finished work, and at eight o'clock—to go to sleep." His father's favorite whistle was the double whistle, which meant work was canceled due to rain or other weather conditions.

There are thousands of families like Pagdilao's in Hawai'i, families that came a long way to shape, not always willingly, the cultural blueprint of these islands. Many of them had hoped to return to their homeland, but most of them never did.

From his back porch in 'Ewa, the young Pagdilao looked up at the sky and watched the future swoop down on his world. "Through the years, I saw everything from the propeller plane to the jet plane pass over our house," he muses. "I saw changes."

Corrugated metal roofs are ubiquitous in Hawai'i, as in these homes from Hāmākua, Hawai'i (left and above), and Kīlauea, Kaua'i (top).

The main house of a four-acre spread in the coffee-plantation uplands of Hōlualoa, Hawai'i, is reflected in the garage studio door (top). The veranda (above) was added on, and the spacious deck (right) overlooking Kona was part of the original structure.

◆◆◆◆◆◆◆◆◆◆◆◆◆◆◆◆◆◆◆◆◆◆◆◆

The Passing of Plantation Life

On tiny Lānaʻi, where forty-five hundred of the original fourteen thousand acres remain in pineapple production, more and more workers are moving into new homes in Lānaʻi City, with better furniture, more space, and different needs. The changes are subtle but profound.

Sol Kahoʻohalahala, a fifth-generation native of Lānaʻi and the director of cultural resources at the island's deluxe hotel, The Lodge at Koele, has come to accept those changes. "We just buried the last of my great-grandmother's generation," he reflects. "She was the last of fourteen children in that generation. As we drove in the procession toward the graveyard, we passed right by the Lodge. It hit me: This was the last *tutu* [grandmother], the last surviving child of one entire generation of people on Lānaʻi. Here went one generation, and here was the new, driving by a symbol of tourism.

"It means we have different circumstances and new things to consider in our lives. It's not negative, it's an acceptance and understanding of where we are, where we've come from, and what lies ahead. It is going to be my life on Lānaʻi, because my *tutus* are all finished here. They left me a lot of good things."

Opposite: This house, formerly a barn, is now a studio filled with Hawaiian collectibles and sculpture. The couch (right) is equipped with mosquito netting, also seen from the deck (top left). The table (bottom left) displays, aptly, a horse.

On the desk (left) is a collection of Hawaiian knickknacks gathered in—of all places—the Pacific Northwest on the mainland.

Some of Hawaiʻi's older Japanese still remember the songs their ancestors sang in the fields from their first days in Hawaiʻi. They were called *hole hole bushi*, after the Hawaiian term for dried sugarcane leaves. "When I left Yokohama, I cried as I sailed alone," goes one song. "But now I have children here, and grandchildren, too."

Cattle ranching is number five in Hawai'i's diversified agriculture today, but it is much more than an industry. Like plantations, it was a non-native tradition that took root in the nineteenth century and held firm through the years, enriching the island culture as it

became its own unique hybrid of Hawaiian and western ways. Even the word *paniolo* rolls off the tongue like an easygoing riff from a Spanish guitar. The Hawaiian version of the word *español*, the word *paniolo* conjures up an entire cultural milieu, the romantic image of stalwart, hardworking, nature-loving men riding and roping in this tropical state's most rugged and unlikely profession. **H**awai'i's ranch houses

are modest, eclectic, and, in

the words of one inveterate rancher, "absolutely unfussy—meant to be knocked about." This model of utility leaves the architectural stereotype—of the rambling ranch house with the low-pitched roof and Spanish Colonial details—to Hawai'i's mainland counter

Paniolo

parts. In the Islands, where ranches occupy everything from torrid plains to velvety upcountry meadowlands, ranch style is functional and adaptable. "A dog and a cat live here, too, and they bring in mud and cow manure and I can't worry about it," declares a longtime Big Island rancher with characteristic grit.

The modesty and lack of ceremony notwithstanding, Hawai'i's ranch homes house some of the finest examples in existence of early Hawaiian cabinetry and rare native woods. Kitchens of *koa*, a large mimosa-like hardwood unique to the Hawaiian Islands, and dairies with slate roofs appeared in some of the earliest ranches in the Islands, a testament to the resourcefulness and craftsmanship that characterized this genre from the beginning. Hawai'i's most venerable ranch homes were built decades ago, many of them in remote, inhospitable areas.

One such domicile, at Kohala Nui Farms on Hawai'i island, is a composite of three plantation homes that were hauled over a mud track to a vantage point on a knoll, then pieced together into a classic ranch home—charming, creative, and resourceful. A veranda wraps around the assemblage like an open-air enclosure; wrapped snugly within, the house peers out over the veranda to sweeping panoramas of Maui and the North Kohala hills. The backdrop is a constantly changing pattern of light, moisture, and movement as fine mountain mists alternate with sunlight.

"It's just thrown together," the owner says, shrugging modestly. "I've only had electricity here for the last ten years. There are no things that match; it's just an old shack with a tin roof on it. It doesn't have a plan, it just grows."

The rugged, casual, pioneering style befits a tradition that was planted in Hawai'i's outdoors long before most other commercial ventures were even heard of. Ranching had its beginnings in Hawai'i three or four decades before many of the western states, and Hawai'i's *paniolo* were kicking up the dust before the American West was born. Years before California, Texas, and the Pacific Northwest became a part of the United States, Hawaiians were riding, roping, herding, and breeding cattle on Hawai'i island.

At two thousand feet high in North Kohala, this is a house of windows, verandas, and, thus, light-filled rooms, like the kitchen (right). The owner can see every paddock from virtually every room. The ranch features a tank for storing the water (above right) that must be pumped up a steep hill.

A saddle rests in Hāwī (left), sheep graze in Waimea (top), and children learn the ropes (above).

Opposite: Scenes from Waimea, Hawai'i island, the home of the Parker Ranch.

The First Ranches

Their lives astride began when the British captain George Vancouver brought the first cattle to Hawai'i island in 1793—ten years before the first horses arrived—as a gift for Kamehameha I. Vancouver considered ranching a future alternative to sandalwood, a profitable crop but one destined for eventual depletion. Kamehameha declared a ten-year *kapu*, or taboo, on the slaughter of these cattle, thereby fomenting the proliferation of wild bullocks and the eventual commercialization of leather and meat products. There were not only the sandalwood traders to accommodate, there were the whalers and the traders in furs, spices, teas, and silks. By the 1820s, there was a significant market for beef, tallow, and hides for the numerous ships seeking provisions.

One of those sandalwood ships carried John Palmer Parker, the Horatio Alger of ranching in Hawai'i. A sailor from New England, Parker went from sailing to the shipping business and, by 1815 and his second visit to Hawai'i, had become caretaker of the king's royal fishponds. Before long, he was a hunter nonpareil of wild bullocks, and then one of the first private ranchers in Hawai'i, with landholdings that multiplied apace and a reputation that wouldn't stop as Hawai'i's premier cattle baron and *paniolo*.

With his Hawaiian wife Rachel Kipikane, a chiefess and descendant of Kamehameha I, Parker was instrumental in establishing the *paniolo* tradition in Hawai'i. To his initial two acres—bought from Kamehameha III for a token ten dollars—were added 640 acres granted to his wife because of her noble birth. The New England–style home they built out of *koa* was named Mānā, and the seeds of their ranching dynasty were irrevocably sown.

From the beginning, the ranching tradition they established was a combination of cultures. Hawai'i's *paniolo* learned their skills from the Indian, Spanish, and Mexican *vaqueros* who arrived in Hawai'i in the 1830s at the behest of Kamehameha III, the same king who gave Parker his two acres of land. Descending upon the Islands in their full western regalia, the *vaqueros* taught the Hawaiians how to handle the wild bullocks that were running amok in the native forests and *taro* fields. The *vaqueros* brought their skills, music, and self-sufficient outdoor lifestyle, incorporated them with the Hawaiian ways, and planted the seeds of what has become one of Hawai'i's oldest and most colorful industries.

The Hawai'i Cowboy

Yutaka Kimura, one of Hawai'i's most prominent cowboys, witnessed a large part of the development of ranching in his fifty years with the Big Island's Parker Ranch, the ranching dynasty founded by John Parker. With 50,000 head of cattle on 225,000 acres sprawling from the ocean to 8,000 feet high on the slopes of Mauna Kea, Parker Ranch is the country's largest under individual ownership. Kimura worked for many years under A. W. Carter, the manager responsible for diversifying ranch operations as early as the turn of the century. Racehorses, sheep, hogs, corn, bees, and dairy and poultry operations also became a part of the ranch under Carter's progressive management, and other ranches followed suit.

"He was the one who tried to raise cattle and better the breed," explains Kimura, who started working on the ranch in 1918. "In the early 1900s they slowly began importing cattle from the mainland and New Zealand. Carter discovered that the most ideal, easy-to-raise cattle were Herefords. By 1935, the ranch was one of the largest all-Hereford-breed cattle ranches in the world."

At eighty-five years old, Kimura is a testament to the salutary effects of the *paniolo* life. He has only recently stopped riding a horse, and he's seen some changes in the cowpunching business. "I worked with many old cowboys," he reflects with pride. "In those days, *paniolo* were tough people. They could take the punishment, ride the horse all day, go through rain and wind and cold from before the sun comes up to way after dark. It's not an easy life; even today, most nationalities can't take it."

The contemporary *paniolo* wears a baseball cap and, where the terrain allows it, uses a Jeep or a motorbike to drive cattle. On the Big Island's Kahuā Ranch, the Honda motorcycles used for roundup are referred to as the "Japanese quarterhorse." In the old days, *paniolo* had to rope, brand, raise cattle, wean them, swim them through shark-infested waters to waiting ships for export, and make rigorous cattle drives through changing terrain and microclimates.

Hawaiians took readily to the rigors of ranching. In the Big Island's Kona and Kohala districts, four ranches—Huʻehuʻe, Puʻuwaʻawaʻa, Kahuā, and Parker Ranch itself—are or were owned by cousins who were the part-Hawaiian descendants of John Parker. The Hawaiians in ranching were often people of chiefly rank, and even today, the Hawaiians and part-Hawaiians absorbed into their labor pool are among the few Islanders still able to visit the places where their ancestors lived and played.

Ferrier Henry Silva (right), who braids from a garage post while standing up, makes saddles and *paniolo* gear in his tack shed in Kula, Maui. Saddles and rawhide take shape (below, left and right).

Life as a Paniolo

Ranching's gone from wild bullock hunters to a modern industry, with feedlots, artificial insemination, good veterinary medicine, scientific grass management, water pumping, erosion control, and quality beef breeding," explains Dr. Brysson Greenwell, whose great-grandfather, one of Hawai'i island's early ranchers, settled in Kona in 1853. "In the old days, the cowboys had to handle and tame the cattle as well as mend fences and stone walls and tend to the pipelines and water tanks." Water pumps were eventually introduced and well water was pumped from sea level thousands of feet upslope to feed the cattle, with water catchment tanks augmenting the supply. In the dry Kona region, water was a major consideration in ranching and bad times usually meant droughts and forest fires.

"There were dairies scattered around as well, and the Hawaiians and Portuguese who lived in the mountains had milk cows," he explains. "They'd make butter, wrap it in wax paper, hollow out a banana stalk, fill it with the butter, and ship it to Honolulu for market. In those days our ranches had butter, wool, oranges, and an old country store that sold hardtack and dry goods."

Greenwell grew up on one of the three Greenwell ranches that at one time occupied thirty-five thousand acres from one end of Kona to the other. His father, Jack Greenwell, still runs the small Circle-J Ranch, although the once-large family enterprise diminished considerably in the 1980s. Brysson Greenwell remembers his *paniolo* childhood with fondness.

"The style of living was that of a country gentleman who had a few servants and a few employees, and who lived simply," Greenwell recalls. "There was no TV, they played cards, went to church, raised families, and worked long hours. None of my ancestors was lazy.

"The older large ranches were somewhat like plantations.

They were founded by people with some money, and they were patriarchal. All of the people, including the owners and those who worked on the ranch, lived and died there. When the old-timers became too old to work, they were given a home and taken care of forever."

Hawai'i's old ranch houses were built in separate units, called outbuildings, to accommodate the diverse activities of the *paniolo* life. There was the main house, a bathhouse, a kitchen (or cook house), a laundry house, butter house, guest cottage, and out-house. The cook house was generally built away from the main house as a safety precaution against fire, a common hazard of the time. At the Big Island's Kahuā Ranch, the saddle house is one of

Opposite: Snow-capped Mauna Loa looms behind the *mauka* ranch house of Kealakekua Ranch, Ltd. Above left: An English heritage is remembered with pictures of royalty above the fireplace. Above: Hats, bells, and a cow skull.

The view from 3,000 feet above sea level looks over the 9,000-acre Kahuā Ranch in North Kohala, the Big Island. At sunset the green palette changes to violets and reds.

the last ranch units still operating in a complex that includes century-old components.

The 9,000-acre Kahuā Ranch raises cattle, sheep, and carnations in the carpeted greenness of the Kohala Mountains, thousands of feet above sea level. The animals graze placidly in some of Hawai'i's most picturesque terrain, and windmills whir constantly as a source of alternative energy. The aroma of fresh cookies wafts through the ranch before the cowboys' lunch even hits the table. The main house, at a 3,250-foot altitude, is an attractive amalgam of parts that have been added on, moved around, and built upon for as long as a hundred years. In the days

of railroads and seaports, lumber had to be hauled up by wagon. Although the functions of Kahuā's outbuildings eventually became centralized under one roof, the carpenter's shop, servants' quarters, washhouse, chapel, and saddle house are still sprinkled throughout the tree-shaded grounds.

Brysson Greenwell's childhood memories center around a similar kind of ranch house—a classic *mauka* (mountain) home called Pu'ulehua, located ten miles upslope from the ranch headquarters. It burned down in a forest fire, but not before the Greenwells had enjoyed many a summer in the warm glow of its ancient fireplace, cooking large pots of savory stews on its antique wood stove.

"It was full of antique furniture, and we'd often stay there for

weeks or months at a time," Greenwell reminisces. "There was a fireplace in the main house, and the kitchen was made of solid *koa*—*koa* walls and floors, with two long benches on either side of the table, which was covered with oilcloth.

"We'd ride up there on horses, with mules carrying our clothes, food provisions, roof iron, lumber, and salt to put out for the cattle. We'd gather at five in the morning, before daylight, each with a cloth rice bag filled with clothes. The littlest children had to be carried by a cowboy. It took us three hours to get there."

The summer entourage included two cows, which were driven up as a source of milk and cream. Sugar, flour, rice, and hardtack (Hilo Saloon Pilot crackers) went up with the family. Meat hung on hooks in the open air (there was no refrigeration),

and hunting for wild sheep and pigs augmented the culinary offerings.

"The cowboys were Hawaiians, part-Hawaiians, Portuguese, Filipinos, Japanese, *haole* combinations," continues Greenwell. "The men, separated at times from their families, who lived down the hill, went home on weekends."

The day began early, with a breakfast of hot stew and rice to warm the workers in the chill mountain air. Then off they would ride, with sandwiches and rice balls packed snugly in their denim lunch bags, to spend a day taming cattle, repairing fences and water tanks, and removing the noxious plants that had become hazardous environmental intruders. Cattle had to be branded and earmarked, and the males castrated and let out with their mothers. Eventually

they would be weaned from them and raised as beef stock. Horses, too, needed to be broken and tamed, and no one came home until the jobs were done.

If there was any shred of daylight left, a rousing game of croquet, volleyball, badminton, or softball kept the children and cowboys in action. At night, the family and workers huddled around the fireplace or flickering kerosene lamps and played music or a game of cards. A Hawaiian game called *kāmau*, much like trumps, was favored almost as much as the wildly exaggerated tales of hunting and wilderness exploits that were the *paniolo* signature. Finally, each person would take a turn at easing luxuriously into a soothing, hot bath in a large galvanized tub filled with water heated by the wood stove.

John Parker's original home in Waimea, called Mānā Hale, was much like a wooden saltbox, built of *koa* with a steep slate roof and surrounded by saw pits and heaps of *koa* lumber harvested from the adjacent forests. The scent of sandalwood infused the night air from tubs of burning coal, and the spartan, gleaming furniture complemented the purity of the building materials, materials that included nails made from the same *koa* trees that peppered the land.

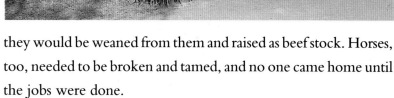

Outbuildings at Kahuā Ranch include a saddle house, carpenter shop, guest cottages (above left and right), and a chapel (right). Opposite: A Border collie enjoys the panoramic view of the Kohala hills...backyard gardens...and an entrance shaded by *hāpu'u* ferns.

Cowhides line the dining-room floor (above) of the Kahuā Ranch house. Next to the lava-rock fireplace (opposite right) are Hawaiian stone implements that were found on the property.

Opposite: Double-woven *lauhala* mats, nineteenth-century *koa* furniture by Henry and William Weeks, and a Pilipo Springer painting enliven the living room (above) of the Mahealani Ranch. The silk brocade chairs (left) belonged to Princess Bernice Pauahi Bishop.

The Modern Ranch

Like the *paniolo* shelter, the style of living has changed considerably since pioneer times. The ranches that remain in remote, hard-to-traverse terrain still use horses for roundup, but most have adopted the use of Jeeps and trucks. Mechanization, more sophisticated grazing methods, and the practice of raising cattle for feeders have brought necessary advancements in an industry of rising costs and diminishing returns.

"A modern rancher sits in an office and pushes a pencil and keeps the books. A working rancher gets dirty," asserts Barbara Nobriga, a fourth-generation rancher who owns, with her husband, Edwin, the Mahealani Ranch in Kawanui, North Kona. "At our ranch, like most others, we have diversified. We are in real estate, rentals, and we build and sell. I also teach horsemanship and board horses.

"Ranching has become more mechanized, yes, but as a way of caring for cattle, it's basically the same. You still brand them at a certain time each year, you still change your pastures, and you still put your bulls in and pull them out at the same time. Where you see the change is in the use of machinery and the less frequent use of horses. Everyone's looking for time-savers now."

The Nobrigas still use horses to round up cattle—not only because they love and board horses and give lessons in horsemanship, but also because the open terrain of their six-hundred-acre ranch is too rugged for vehicles. Their children, involved in all aspects of the business, were taught the complete skills in horsemanship and ranching, and their grandchildren are the sixth generation to be raised in the same place and in the same *paniolo* tradition. Now there are the amenities of automobiles, telephones, and electricity, but there are still chickens, and cats, dogs, a pet pig named Boots, cattle roaming the hills, and milk cows to care for.

"We can make fresh butter and whipped cream , and what the

kids enjoy more than ever is making fresh ice cream," Nobriga notes proudly. "It's better than Häagen-Dazs." Their pet pig before Boots drank champagne from a crystal goblet; Boots roots out chocolate truffles from under the Christmas tree and entertains guests year-round.

The board-and-batten ranch house has lava-rock pillars (right) and wild jungle fowl (opposite) with tails that can reach thirty inches.

The "good, clean, outdoor living," as Barbara Nobriga calls it, centers around their rambling, gracious five-bedroom board-and-batten home, also called Mahealani. Built by Nobriga's grandparents in 1903, Mahealani is perched fifteen hundred feet above sea level, in the saddle between Hualālai and Mauna Loa mountains in the Big Island's North Kona District.

The *paniolo* tradition took root here when ranchers Eliza and William F. Roy, Barbara Nobriga's great-grandparents, built their home in the mid-1800s a stone's throw from where the Nobrigas' house now stands. They raised ten children and enjoyed several decades there before Eliza Roy died in 1907. The house remained vacant until Nobriga's grandparents revitalized and reopened it in 1912 as the Wall Hotel, which quickly became an oasis for some of Hawai'i's most celebrated visitors of the time.

The Wall Hotel may be gone now, but the *paniolo* lifestyle has continued unabated at this ranching homestead in the mountains. It is the center of life for three generations of contemporary Big Island *paniolo* who inherited, and have continued, a style of working and living increasingly difficult to maintain. Brysson Greenwell, now in his fifties, recalls being told at an early age that it would be difficult for him to have a future in ranching.

"My father told me that because of the growth of our family, not all of us could stay on the ranch in managerial positions. I would have stayed there if I could have had a good position, but in the end it was wise of me to choose my own profession."

Greenwell went on to become a surgeon in Honolulu but remains the raconteur and archivist in a clan that remains close to its roots. "In my family, we have all kinds of people, from

helicopter pilots to schoolteachers and doctors. It was my father's generation that were the ranchers and retired ranchers. It's my generation that's seeing the transition, with the ranching economy becoming more complex and less viable, more ranch lands being sold, and people spreading further and further into other ways of life," he muses. "I think there's a sadness, a sense of loss, because of the inexorable changes dictated by economics and taxes."

The inflated value of land in Hawai'i has contributed to the difficulties of passing ranches on to offspring, or even continuing the business. In the words of one rancher, "It's hard to make a dollar on a ranch." Astronomical property and estate taxes often necessitate the sale of ranch lands to high-paying developers. With resort development perched on their doorstep, more than a few ranchers have found themselves millionaires before the mud on their boots has even dried. Some ranches, like Kualoa on O'ahu,

have devoted a part of their operations to tourist activities such as horseback riding and water sports.

Although ranch lands are being viewed more and more as real estate, much of the land can't be used for anything else. Along with the demand for beef, that fact guarantees a small margin of stability in an uncertain future. The Parker Ranch produces 10 million pounds of beef a year, totaling one-third of the state's beef production, and even they have diversified and launched tour programs. According to Brent Buckley, a beef cattle specialist with the University of Hawaii College of Tropical Agriculture and Human Resources, there are 150 to 200 working ranches in Hawai'i and hundreds of other, smaller backyard operations.

Children duck around the corners of this 1903 home (below), the headquarters for six generations.

Opposite: The Big Island's Mahealani Ranch boards horses and teaches horsemanship.

Horses and Trees

The ranching presence is also indelibly imprinted upon Hawai'i's cultural landscape. Every July 4, rodeos kick up the dust in towns like Makawao, Maui, and every major parade throughout the year features spirited *paniolo* and the sweeping drama of the *pā'ū* riders, women sitting astride with their long, voluminous, distinctively wrapped skirts of blinding satins and velvets.

At these festive affairs, *paniolo* legends like Yutaka Kimura don their best cowboy boots and finely woven, lei-bedecked *lauhala* hats to join the parade on horseback. The parades bring out the best in *paniolo* regalia, reminding Kimura of the days when the dusty, sweaty, rough-and-tumble *paniolo* put their weathered hands to the earth and became artists in a delicate medium.

"When I was younger, Waimea had a lot of flowers everywhere," Kimura recalls. "When we'd ride to different stations up in the mountains, we men would find wild grass and flowers in the pastures and braid the strands into leis. The leis would go around our hats, and even when they were dry, we still wore them. When we rode back to Waimea village, everyone looked at our hats and admired."

There is no better portrayal of the *paniolo* way than the life and writings of Armine von Tempski, in whose imagination every scent, sound, and gentle *paniolo* pondering sprang to life in delicious detail. In her book *Born in Paradise*, she describes her father, Haleakalā Ranch manager Louis von Tempski, as larger than life, "the super-*paniolo* heading the goodly company of booted and spurred men who went out and came in like a vast tide at the beginning and end of each day. He was horses and trees, the blue magnificence of Haleakalā. He was Hell, Damn, and By-Golly. He rode racehorses and roped wild bulls. He played polo, danced, and sang (*sic*) *hulas*. . . . When people were happy, they came to celebrate with him."

"**O**cean people are different from land people. The ocean never stops saying and asking into ears, which don't sleep like eyes. . . . Sometimes ocean people are given to understand the newness and oldness of the world; then all morning they try to keep that boundless joy like a little sun inside their chests."—Maxine Hong Kingston, *China Men*

The Hawaiian language describes the sea in countless ways. Traditional Hawaiians have names for waters along the coast, the open ocean, the shore break, the shallow sea, the sea within the reef, the dark sea, the sea for wading, the sea for bathing naked. Every fishing hole has a name. The dark blue sea has a name. *Kai malino*—the calm sea. *Kai ke'oke'o*—the sea of white water. *Kai 'ula'ula*, the sea of red, and *kai kuehu*, waves crashing against cliffs. Even waves have their own specific nomenclature. Sunken waves, billowing waves, waves that swirl sand, waves that break on one side—each has its own term that captures its meaning vividly. **K**ai is the word

Makai

for sea, and *makai* is one of the few Hawaiian words still in use.

Mauka, meaning "toward the mountain," and *makai*, meaning "toward the sea," are important directional aids in Hawai'i, more commonly used than north, south, east, and west. In Hawai'i, one travels and lives around the islands, *mauka* or *makai*, leeward or windward, in the valleys or in the heights. The orientations of *makai* and *mauka* are a throwback to the ancient method of dividing land into parcels of land, often pie-shaped, that extended from the sea to the uplands.

Today *makai* is also a style of living, and it is evocative of many things. Instead of lyrical Hawaiian names, ocean sites and surf breaks may carry such modern-day monikers as Gums, Pipeline, Backyards, Point Panic, Slaughterhouse, Gas Chambers, Rice Bowl. . . . *Makai* style is all of these, but it is also the salubrious salt air, sails and whales in the distance, sand on concrete floors, an appetite for barbecues. Bathing suits drying on car antennas. Fins and body boards strewn across the lawn. Gathering shells and fishing balls in the pink of dawn. Scanning the horizon for porpoises. *Makai* style is also the bittersweet moment when shadows have gathered in the footsteps in the sand, and it's time for beachgoers to go home.

When you don't have to go home, when you are already at home on the beach, that's the ultimate *makai* style. "Our family is always amazed that the Pacific Ocean is our front yard," marvels Marta Sanburn at her Portlock, O'ahu, home. "We're made constantly aware of all the navigation going on around us, the canoe races and sailing. Our own children are a part of it. They have surfed in our front yard, and we've sailed in our front yard. . . ."

Rampant resort and private development along Hawai'i's shore-line has made the classic Hawaiian beach home a next-to-endangered species. Kāhala, once a haven for the *kama'āina* and one of O'ahu's most fashionable *makai* areas, has been virtually dismantled under the weight of nouveau beach dwellers and their showy replacements of concrete and tile. "One area we're losing fast is the beach cot-

Named Kahiwawai, sacred waters, this picturesque ocean-front home in Kealakekua, Hawai'i, is known for its brilliant sunsets.

tage," notes a Honolulu architect ominously. "Look at what's disappearing in Kāhala. The classic two-bedroom beach cottages are turning into ten-bedroom estates. It's the changing face of Kāhala, and the pressures of real estate."

Such pressures notwithstanding, beach dwellers in Hawai'i live the life most people dream about, a life lived close to the elements. The vibrations of nearby waves roaring through a house carry a thrill bordering on fear. A measure of surrender is called for here; the surroundings define the house. Many *makai* homes in high-surf areas are elevated, a safeguard against the gargantuan waves that have been known to sweep houses away without warning. Residents of the North Shore, O'ahu, have anecdotes galore about the hazard of high surf and the precautions necessary in the winter. "It was about fifty feet," recalls North Shore resident Alice Tracy in describing the wave that took her beach cottage in February of 1986. "It came in the middle of the night, at twelve-thirty. The guest in the cottage, a writer from San Francisco, woke up to find himself floating out into the yard on his mattress." That cottage was devastated by the wave; its replacement was built a full story above the ground. Others describe similar events surrounding high winter surf or *tsunami* (tidal waves) that have scattered telephone poles, boulders, trees, seaweed, fish, and the entire spectrum of ocean detritus in garages, yards, and living rooms.

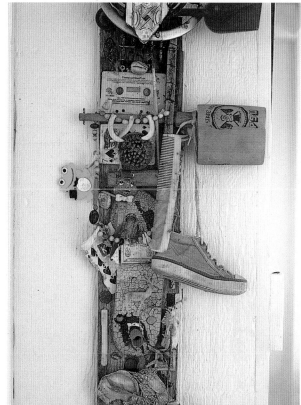

Opposite: The seawall, which is repaired yearly, is the only protection for this plantation-style beach house on Kealakekua Bay.

A cement slab floor and modern amenities (above), and collectibles from the beach and childhood mementos (right).

Opposite: The Dickey roofline appears through the trees at this south Maui wooden beach home designed by architect Bert Ives.

Corner details (right) and a pair of designer *koa* rockers only a few feet from the beach (below).

The Beach Indoors

Safety and protection are a part of *makai* style, but so is an openness to the elements. Exposure to the sea is de rigueur in *makai* style. A *lānai* facing the sunrise or sunset, windows that open to the sea, generous ocean views, and the liberal circulation of salt air are the distinctive features of an oceanfront home. Most of these homes have outdoor showers, and the more casual of them eschew carpets for timeless floorings that can endure the endless inflow of sandy feet.

Homes on the windward side of the island often receive stiff, salt-laden onshore winds that deposit crystals of salt on windows and fixtures. Windbreaks help—ironwood trees are popular—but they also block the view. An unobstructed view has its price if the house lies directly in the path of the salty trade winds. High maintenance is required, for salt creates corrosion. Gardens are especially vulnerable. Even on the North Shore of O'ahu, where offshore winds are the rule, houses and gardens are battered in the winter months. "We're across the street from the beach, but we still get the full force of the salt air," remarks longtime North Shore resident Josephine Carvalho. "During winter, our place is completely brown. The leaves and plants and flowers turn brown with the sea breeze blowing day and night. It's that way all the way up the shoreline, from Hale'iwa to Kahuku."

Opposite: The classic North Shore surfer's pad is choked with posters, maps, fins, shorts, and surfboards. Space is used efficiently in this home, once a tiny tool shed near Sunset Beach and Backyards.

Right: In addition to their traditional use, neon-colored surfboards function as flamboyant decorative accessories, both inside and out.

◆ ◆

Home on the Waves

Makai homes range from opulent estates in Portlock, Diamond Head, and Lanikai to surfboard-choked shacks on the North Shore, where surfers are likely to spend more time in the ocean than at home. One such surfer's haven is a color-splashed house the size of a toolshed, where a recorded message boasts to callers, "I am in the ocean. . . .You are on the phone." "The winds are outrageous and the surf is one to three . . ." reports the recorder on another day.

"It used to be called the 'banana shack,'" explains surfer and contractor Jeff Johnson, the former owner who built the house. "It was built as a construction shack from materials left over from other jobs." To the original eight-by-ten-foot room with cedar walls were added a bathroom and kitchen, abundant window space, and neon-bright surfboards in every corner. Located in the backyard of a surf spot called Backyards, the house makes efficient use of space and color and expresses the inherent freedom of the surfing life.

"There were ironwoods and bushes where the house is now," continues Johnson. "Going there always feels like being on an outer island. The best thing about living near the ocean is that you can get in the water every day. In the end, the house, to a surfer, is just a place to sleep; it gives you the basic amenities.'"

Johnson lives near the world-famous Pipeline, at a spot called Gums—so named because a surfboard embedded with a set of teeth washed in one day at that spot. Similarly ghostly tales haunt the North Shore beaches where some of the legends of surfing have mysteriously disappeared. Even benign bays and harbors have a roster of rescue stories to be told. At Maunalua Bay on the southern shore of O'ahu, few will forget the dramatic rescue of Talbott, the Sanburns' 175-pound Saint Bernard.

It began prosaically enough, with the loyal dog following her masters as they sailed their Hobie out to sea. The Hobie turned back, but the dog kept going until, with ten minutes left in her, she was rescued by a fishing boat coming in from Moloka'i.

"She was in deep water," recounts Marta Sanburn. "When the fishermen spotted her, they thought she was a seal. Someone said, 'We don't have seals on O'ahu.' They finally figured out she was a dog, and it took them quite a while to get her aboard." Talbott was eventually brought in to Hawai'i Kai, where two young girls adopted her and spectators plied her with food. A trip to the Yacht Club reunited the dog with her family, and they lived to talk about it.

For intrepid surfer Jeff Johnson, the highlight of a lifetime spent on the beach was the fortuitous sighting of humpback whales as they mated in the open ocean. "It was phenomenal," he recalls. "The two whales remained on the surface, and you could see two pectoral fins raised the entire time. They were slapping the water, as if to balance themselves and stay together. This went on for four or five minutes,

Windows and sliding doors line the entire front of this forty-five-year-old classic beach home in Portlock, O'ahu (left and opposite top). Opposite, below left: The dining room overlooks Maunalua Bay and the eastern flank of Diamond Head. Opposite, below right: Lloyd Sexton prints on a trellis wall.

and we could see it all clearly from the beach." Even if he never uncovers his fortune by swimming, as he hopes, into a clump of ambergris (the valuable whale secretion used in perfumery), Johnson will be well endowed with the riches of the sea.

The Silent Sea

On the windward side of the island, where the sun rises out of the ocean and waves rarely exceed two feet, the rhythm of the day is different. Residents of Lanikai, an upscale, close-knit windward Oʻahu community, don't see whales mating or fifty-foot waves, but they witness the daily spectacle of sunrise casting a surreal gold-pink glow on the nearby Mokulua Islands. Mokulua means "two islands together," and today the two—Moku Nui, the bigger island, and Moku Iki, the smaller—are state bird sanctuaries. In the old days, each end of Lanikai beach contained a Hawaiian fishing shrine that was used to appease the fishing gods and pinpoint fishing areas offshore. As you look out to the east—the *kūkulu hikina*, where the sun rises—from this snowy stretch of sand, or if you look out to sea from the perimeter of any of the Hawaiian Islands, the serenity and power call to mind what the ancients felt of the sea. "The ocean was one of the gods," writes Grady Timmons in his book *Waikiki Beachboy*. "It was a source of protein, a field for sport, a sanctuary. It was a friend, not an adversary, and perhaps for this reason the ancient Hawaiians were in tune with its mysteries. Living on islands, the Hawaiians were surrounded, defined, sustained, and renewed by the ocean."

ʻŌhiʻa logs shipped from Hawaiʻi island, doors carved in Bali, woven bamboo ceilings, and floors of marble and Balinese teak make up this two-acre, seven-bedroom, ten-bath, seven-structure Polynesian-style complex in Lanikai, windward Oʻahu.

Opposite: Curved walls and large proportions are reminiscent of whales. The monkeypod steps (far right) are made from a tree found on the property, and the banister is made of laminated *koa*.

Humor and South Pacific and nautical themes are evident in Don and Josie Over's dining room "chandelier" (top), the carved Tahitian fertility-god posts in a bedroom (above), and a hand-sewn Tahitian quilt in the guest room (right).

Opposite: The Banzai Pipeline is at the doorstep of this home on the North Shore, O'ahu. The master bath, kitchen, and indeed all the rooms in the house, face the ocean.

111

Cold is a precious commodity in Hawai'i. Many who have spent their lives at sea level find themselves hastening on their getaways to the uplands, where the chill wind upon the cheek and the whiff of wood smoke in the air become seductions they can't resist. Shedding their rubber thongs for boots and their neon bikinis for down parkas, they become, irrevocably, *mauka* dwellers. *Mauka*—toward the mountain—is where life revolves around the simple pleasures: a glowing fire, white Cherokee roses festooning the wilds, watsonia in the spring, quaint cabins bordered by hydrangeas, lichen-covered wooden shingles. *Mauka* living comes with its own set of smells, tastes, wildlife, insects, and anecdotes, all peculiar to the region and each a testament to the powerful allure of the hinterlands. "Upcountry air is always crisp, and the quiet is only interrupted by the chirping of birds, an occasional pheasant squawk, and maybe the flutter of a hang glider's sail heading from Waipoli

Mauka

to Waiakoa," comments Jody Baldwin, a sea-level dweller until she moved in 1972 to Kula, Maui. "You can still charge groceries at the neighborhood store here. You can smell the strong fragrance of lemon eucalyptus all around, and freshly chopped firewood. I wake up early to pink mornings and purple jacarandas."

Looking *mauka* from where Baldwin lives, you can see Haleakalā's rolling pastures and pine and redwood forests undulating down 10,023 feet of hillside. Looking *makai*, the sweeping view encompasses Mā'alaea Bay, Kahului Bay, and the central Maui isthmus that joins them, with its patchwork fields of sugarcane and pineapple. The view can be seen from every room in Baldwin's house.

In Volcano on Hawai'i island, the primordial outpourings of Kīlauea Volcano have attracted a community of artists who say they are inspired, nurtured, and creatively sustained by the activities of Pele, the volcano goddess, and the phenomenon of the land creating and re-creating itself. In Kula (invariably considered "upcountry" rather than *mauka*) and in Waimea on the Big Island, flower and vegetable farms blanket the hillsides with color, a crazy-quilt testimonial to the fecundity of volcanic soil. Throughout the major islands of Hawai'i, small communities along the ridges of *mauka* regions are smothered by bamboo forests, guava trees, wild avocados, and the rapturous fragrance of wild gingers and night-blooming jasmine. Frequently in upcountry areas, petals of jacaranda dust the streets and lawns with a layer of lavender, and the brooding mountains cast shadows on the lowlands. In areas more remote, such as the four-thousand-foot-high Kōke'e, Kaua'i, a wrenching beauty prevails—a world of soaring white-tailed tropic birds, riotous *lehua* blossoms, rare and endangered native flora, dappled trails, and the bleating of wild goats ricocheting against surreal canyon walls.

Immersed in this beauty, a *mauka* house could be anything from a rugged, relocated plantation home to a chalet, a Tudor home, or an old ranch house with rooms added on through the generations. Shelter from the changing upland elements—fog, wind, rain, an occasional frost, and the piercing cold of the winter months—is de rigueur in a *mauka* house. Wide eaves, verandas, and wraparound gardens are aesthetic and functional, allowing outdoor enjoyment in benign conditions and a cocoon of protection at all times. And when the sun shines, it hardly matters; you're out hiking in the wilderness anyway.

Halemanu, the most renowned house in Kōke'e, was built in 1867 as a ranch house, added to for two more generations, and dismantled, timber by timber, for a move downhill to Kōloa in 1985. There it stands, rebuilt, on the property of Kaua'i *kama'āina* Valdemar Knudsen, grandson of the rancher and pioneer who built it. "My grandfather took his new wife up to Kōke'e in 1867, and she fell in love with the place," explains Knudsen. "The reason the mountain house was developed was because my grandmother found it was too hot in the lowlands, where my grandfather was raising cattle and sugar. She found it was lovely and stimulating to go up to the 3,500-foot elevation. They'd stay there for months at a time; she raised her family up in Kōke'e."

Knudsen remembers running twenty-five to thirty mares and a couple of studs the fifteen-mile distance from the lowlands to Kōke'e, where they became surefooted mountain horses used for ranching and recreation. "We used to ride like wild Indians—people can't do that anymore up there," he laughs. In his grandfather's time, the building materials had to be packed on mules and wagons for the four-hour trek up the hill. "Most of that lumber came from the Pacific Northwest, and a lot of people think they threw it overboard into the ocean, tied it with ropes, and pulled the planks through the salt water to the shore," explains Knudsen. "It seemed to be good treatment for termites. There were no power boats at the time, so they must have done that when the schooners pulled in."

The solarium (above left), master bedroom (left), and every other room in this Kula home have views of a large part of Maui and the West Maui mountains.

Opposite: A historic *mauka* home in Nu'uanu is filled with heirlooms from many generations.

The *koa* bench with its original horsehair mattress (right) and the family pictures of three generations are nostalgic touches in this century-old home in Waimea, Hawai'i. Below: The bathtub has been there since the beginning, the cast-iron stove for seventy-five years, and the one-piece *koa* canoe paddles are from pre-western days.

Living is largely outdoors in Kōke'e, Kaua'i, where the wooden homes reflect a simple lifestyle without television and the usual amenities. At a cool 4,000-foot elevation, the stone fireplace (above) is used often.

Opposite: *Plumeria, ti* leaves, a canoe paddle, and a Ray Jerome Baker photo printed by Boone Morrison reflect the owner's interest in things Hawaiian.

The Wettest Spot

Val Knudsen's grandfather also helped plan the historic journey of Queen Emma, widow of Kamehameha IV, and her retinue of a hundred, to the primordial Alaka'i Swamp in 1871. Alaka'i stretches beyond Kōke'e, into the heady uplands of the 5,148-foot Mount Wai'ale'ale, the wettest spot on earth. The queen was so inspired by the setting that she requested a hula performance in the middle of the wilderness. "It is an antediluvian world of quaking bogs and stunted as well as giantlike vegetation where violets turn into trees, trees into ground shrubs, and every sense you ever had about customary nature is turned upside down," wrote Kathryn Hulme, who retraced the queen's steps, in the January 1965 issue of *The Atlantic*. "Nothing . . . can hold a candle to the muscle- and spirit-stretching experience of climbing up to the Alaka'i and bog-hopping across it from tussock to tussock, over the matted turf that sometimes springs under the feet like a trampoline, sometimes gives way and drops you knee-deep into a black mud gravy of rotted vegetation, which has tremendous suction power when you try to pull out of it."

Only the most adventurous and hardy souls venture into the Alaka'i. "I take my students to a certain place I call my classroom," explains Roselle Bailey, the noted *kumu hula* of Kaua'i. "We go there because it has all the plants we need for hula. I urge my students to plant these rare species around their homes and wherever possible." Indeed, hikers in Kōke'e may unknowingly traipse through glens lined with *'ōlapa, 'a'ali'i, maile, 'ēkaha, pāmoho, palapalai, mokihana, lehua,* and other rare native plants that were, and remain, a significant part of Hawaiian cultural and religious practice. Places like Pu'u Ka Pele, an area in Kōke'e from which the volcano goddess Pele is said to have departed from Kaua'i, still throb with power and antiquity, as does Polihale, a ridge that descends to the coastline. According to Hawaiian lore, Polihale is where the chosen souls of the dead gather to make their leap to the land of Po, the realm of the gods.

Wild Fruit

When not engaged in mysterious or death-defying pursuits, upcountry dwellers are content to stoke their fires, tend their gardens, hike to the vistas, and pick the wild fruit that proliferate. Aletha Kaohi, a lifelong Kaua'i resident whose father was a county caretaker in Kōke'e, has deep affection for the bountiful playground of her youth.

"The smell! Kōke'e always had a particular smell," she remembers. "We used to gather purple *liliko'i* [passion fruit] by the bag, and *lemi-wai*, a sweet fruit the size of a mango, which you don't see anymore, and chiyote, which used to grow wild, and wild avocados and watercress. Everything grew wild. And when the plum season opened, cars would park and camp overnight and everyone would be out picking plums in the morning. We all camped out, and there were many potlucks, and the plums were juicy and tasty."

Local residents looked forward to plum season months in advance, and as soon as it ended, looked forward to the next. Although regeneration efforts have made plum season a thing of the past, Kaua'i residents still travel to Kōke'e as if it were another country. "For local people, it's like going to a mountain retreat in Japan," comments Marsha Erickson, formerly of Volcano and now the director of the Kōke'e Museum. "They consider it very far away, almost like going into another time zone." At least regarding the weather, they're not far

off the mark. What's happening at sea level can be ecosystems away from the weather upcountry, where, says Erickson, weather is literally being formed right in front of you. "Places like Volcano, Haleakalā, and Kōke'e, where the clouds are forming around you, is where the weather patterns begin."

As in Kōke'e, *mauka* houses in Volcano (opposite) and Hōlualoa (right) are modest and functional, with the signature red metal roof. The world's most scenic outhouse (above right), no longer in use, is located at the 1,500-foot-high Kona Hotel, where charming yet inexpensive rooms like this one (right) provide a spectacular view along with the basic amenities.

120

Naming the Winds

◆◆◆◆◆◆◆◆◆◆◆◆◆◆◆◆◆◆◆◆◆◆

Aletha Kaohi's father taught her some of the many Hawaiian names for the winds and elements of the region. "The cold wind, the soft wind, the wet wind—there are all kinds of winds. He talked to the winds and they told him about the weather," recalls his daughter. The Hawaiian lexicon contains sixty-five words for different types of rain, and more for the types of wind, and those who know Kōkeʻe say it is a venue for them all.

Roselle Bailey has also searched for the lost names, places, and elements of the Kōkeʻe wilderness. In the early 1980s, Kaohi's father bequeathed to her two invaluable handwritten journals, dated to 1860,

containing little-known ancient Hawaiian chants, many of them about Kaua'i. Bailey was given the privilege of bringing them out, of putting them to dance, perhaps for the first time. "He entrusted these *oli mele* into my keeping, but not really for my keeping, for my putting them out, breathing life into them again for everyone to enjoy," explains Bailey. The books, written in exquisite penmanship, and one in the hand of an elderly person, contain stories and genealogies connected with ancient place names and people. "Some of the places I don't know and have to find," says Bailey. "There are references to the names of winds, names that aren't used today.

"Take *lolomauna*, a wind from Kekaha that comes off the mountain. It took me a long time to find that particular wind. One day in Kaumakani, I was looking at the town of Kekaha. The wind all around us came from one direction, and this wind from Kekaha blew the wind from a cane fire in the opposite direction. It dawned on me that that was *lolomauna*. Why study the elements? When you put them in relationship to the chant, you understand more about the dance, about the culture."

In early morning and late afternoon, the quality of light in these places becomes beatific, filtering like filaments of substance through *koa*, eucalyptus, and Sugi pines. The lambent light charges the atmosphere with a palpable energy. "The scenery was glorious, and mountains, trees, frolicsome water, and scarlet birds all rioted as if in conscious happiness," wrote Isabella Bird of a mountain trip on Kaua'i, in her book *Six Months in the Sandwich Islands*. "All beautiful things which love damp; all exquisite, tender ferns and mosses; all shade-loving parasites flourish there in perennial beauty." In the lands up *mauka*, green is an essence you can can inhale and almost taste.

The historic Tudor-style Danford home in Kōke'e (left) stands alone in the rugged terrain. Opposite: The sure sign of a *mauka* home is its unobtrusiveness. Homes in Kōke'e, Kaua'i, like these, where no one is allowed to live full-time, blend easily into the wilds.

The Lone Eagle

Marsha Erickson is one of the few full-time residents of Kōke'e, now a 4,345-acre state park where cabins are leased for part-time use only. In Kōke'e there are miles of dirt road, cool mists feeding streams and deep-green forests, and an awe-inspiring network of hiking trails. "At the end of the day in the summer, we sit on the back porch and watch the chickens," comments Erickson. "There's no TV in Kōke'e, so you get a lot of talking and a lot of reading done."

"There's a great deal of isolation there because you're not spending a lot of time in front of the TV, radio, or movies," adds Dan Williamson, an O'ahu resident who owns the historic Danford home, a two-story, English-style manor built in Kōke'e in 1935. "There seems to be a lot of visiting, even among people who don't know each other very well. There's a lot of camaraderie in Kōke'e."

Kaohi's father, William Goodwin, was raised in a grass house, brought up as a Hawaiian, grew gardens of *'ākulikuli* (ice plant) to make leis with, and traversed the countryside on foot. "He played the mandolin throughout Kōke'e and was known for the way he entertained the guests," recalls his daughter. "There were cottages people rented from the county; knowing that Dad would sing, people brought their musical instruments and joined in. There was nothing much to do except make music and sit in front of the fire."

The otherworldly songs of the *'i'iwi* and *'apapane*, the elegant and endangered honeycreepers, ring through the forests from dawn to dusk. For untold years, until it was killed in the blades of a helicopter, a solitary golden eagle found refuge in the wilds of Kōke'e. Its sightings were celebrated, noted, and discussed with fervor, and the many who had never seen it dreamed of the first encounter. "We saw it while hiking along the Waimea Canyon to the Waipo'o Falls, in about 1980," recalls Williamson, one of the fortunate few to have seen the bird. "It was very graceful, flying along the canyons catching the draft, close enough so I knew what it was."

Opposite: On Maui, shingled and metal roofs dot the patchwork countryside of flower and vegetable farms (top). *'Ōhi'a* trees and delphiniums front a classic Volcano *mauka* home (bottom).

The mists of Kōke'e are absent from Hōlualoa, where the weather heats up and cools down suddenly. Residents of the town's most colorful house look down to the ocean, sipping coffee from their own land. Anthuriums in bottles line a back window (right), collections of Mundorff hibiscus prints and hula dolls are sprinkled throughout, and sandals await entrance (below).

Winter in Hawai'i

There are no golden eagles on the islands of Hawai'i and Maui, but there is a phenomenon there enjoyed nowhere else in the archipelago. Snow. Local people thrill to the opportunity of sinking their hands into the soft white mounds or skiing on Mauna Kea, the 13,796-foot behemoth that towers over the island of Hawai'i. Snow atop Mauna Kea is an annual event, and snow on Mauna Loa can be seen often enough, but when Haleakalā on Maui is white, people flock there to enjoy the spectacle. "We had a good surprise one year up on Haleakalā," recalls Hilary Parker, a resident of Kula on the slopes of the fabled Maui mountain. "We woke up one morning to see the mountain covered in white. We played in the snow and made snowmen. People went up with plastic bags or socks on their hands. My children took up the Boogie boards and used them to slide around in the snow. What a great idea!" By the next morning, the snow was gone and Haleakalā re-emerged as evergreen.

Mountain-lover Roger Coryell, a resident of O'ahu, has witnessed just about every possible winter condition at the six-thousand-foot level of Haleakalā, where he and his family have spent nearly every Christmas for the past decade in an isolated three-bedroom state cabin without electricity. For his family, Christmas at the Polipoli Springs State Recreation Area means a refuge from commercialism and an ascent into a rarefied, mysterious world where the weather changes instantaneously and rigorous hiking is rewarded with vistas of astonishing magnificence.

"I've hiked to the tops of all major mountains in Hawai'i," Coryell enthuses. "I have been to the tops of Mauna Kea—about five times before they built the road—Mauna Loa, Hualālai, and Haleakalā. I've hiked up Polipoli, from the eight-thousand-foot level up to the summit of Haleakalā, turned around and hiked back down. It is a *breathtaking* hike. Descending, you're walking down the southwest rift of Haleakalā, with big, deep pits and craters, and lava flows, and cliffs, all looking across the channel, with its shifting beauties and winds, and all of a sudden, from along a line of cinder cones, there's Kaho'olawe, parked in the ocean, with the crescent of Molokini nearby."

Mauka living inevitably entails such thrills and vistas earned by the intrepid, who love nothing more than to end such a day with a long, lingering respite at a blazing fireplace. Like snow and a pleasant chill, a fireplace is the most exotic thing to be found in the sun-drenched tropics of Hawai'i. In *mauka* communities, fern-shrouded cabins harbor fireplaces of faraway materials and solitude to soothe the soul. At the Kīlauea Lodge in Volcano on the Big Island, more than one hundred "aloha stones," including coins, Indian arrowheads, opals, gold, amethyst, and memorabilia representing thirty-two countries, are imbedded in a large fireplace built in 1938 in the spirit of international brotherhood. To this day, guests from all over the world exchange stories while they warm themselves at the hearth.

A plantation house in Ha'ikū, Maui (opposite), has views on all sides. Kula (above right), where jacarandas bloom in the spring, sprawls down Haleakalā. On Haleakalā's southern flank, the Polipoli forest lures the intrepid.

Indoor-outdoor is the way of life in Hawai'i. Plants and flowers are used everywhere—to highlight the garden, cut and arranged in the house, made into leis, worn in the hair, and given as gifts. The climate of the tropics allows gardening—daily gardening, in fact—and the colors of these outdoor canvases are the very colors of Hawai'i's

elements. Blue ginger, jade flowers, and hydrangea bring the sea's hues to the mountains. Red hibiscus and *lehua* are lava in plant form. Bougainvillea tumbling down a hillside, the green of a moss-covered courtyard, the sweetness of a *puakenikeni* tree—the hues and scents imbue life here with a profusion of sensory pleasures. If an arid lava field on Hawai'i island can blossom into a garden, imagine the possibilities in the fertile rain-kissed valleys like Nu'uanu. At

one time filled with Kamehameha's *taro* fields, Nu'uanu is crisscrossed with *'auwai*, or

irrigation ditches, built in the 1800s for *taro*. Today these *'auwai* are ornamental, used as landscaped waterways and ponds around the homes of Nu'uanu Valley.

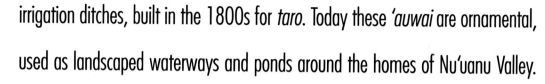

The GARDEN

◆◆◆◆◆◆◆◆◆◆◆◆◆◆◆◆◆◆◆◆◆◆◆

Living in the Garden

When Goodale Moir bought his pie-shaped lot there in the mid-1920s, the subdivision was a bare plain of grass and guava bushes. Completed in 1930, Moir's home was the fifth to be built in the area. As the years passed, the garden, like the valley around it, turned lush, mature, and green, and it melded gracefully with the house it surrounded.

The Moirs named their home Lipolani—loosely translated, "tropical heaven." Its Spanish Colonial design—with tile roof, wide eaves, and walls of plastered hollow tile—holds its own as a stately, distinctive structure that neither overcomes nor is dwarfed by the foliage. Designed by Louis Davis, the house has features that are highly prized today, such as acid-stained concrete floors and stenciled designs embellishing light fixtures, hallway windows, and the dining-room ceiling. Miraculously, the original stenciling has never been retouched in the sixty years since the house was built.

According to May Moir, the architect and craftsmen who built Lipolani had the time and skills to devote to such details. "Lou Davis had worked on the Hawai'i Theatre, and when it was finished, there was a lull before they had to start on the next project," she explains. "To keep the workers busy, they took this job. That's why they painted the ceiling—they had plenty of time, and the skill."

The owner's respect for the land and the home is everywhere evident. It is not a large or showy home; it is a thoughtful oasis in which every color and visual detail has been planned to soothe and refresh. To Moir, an artist, floral designer, and author, the garden is a lifetime project, an ever-evolving canvas. Its temporal function is to provide materials for the flower arrangements she has been creating for the Honolulu Academy of Arts—a forty-year avocation. But the garden, she makes clear, is much more.

"When we came here, I felt very strongly about this property. I could see the possibilities," Moir continues. "I wanted the garden to be a private courtyard. The architect was very well aware of the placing of the elements of the house. He came up here many times before building, under many types of conditions, to see which way the rain fell and the wind was blowing."

The front door faces east and is protected from rain, and the rest of the house is surrounded by patios or exterior garden walls. As soon as those walls went up, the curtains indoors came down and the light, fragrances, and colors streamed in to complement the interior.

The open-air, walled patio adjoining the living room is actually a greenhouse, with social functions as well. Peppered with graceful sprays of phalaenopsis orchids, it is enclosed completely and ventilated in every direction. The glass louvers are removed in May to permit complete ventilation through the summer; in November, to protect the greenhouse from the wind and rain, the louvers are reinstalled. These controls give Moir the freedom to work in any kind of weather. "And when we have parties," she notes, "it's where the bar is. It works well there, because people come in, head for the bar, and then are usually enticed to go further. We can have a hundred people here and you'd never know it, because half of them are in the garden." The patio leads out to a soothing moss garden bordered with hāpu'u ferns, *ti*, and blue gingers that show off their blooms in the summer.

A Javanese wooden mobile and a rare acid-stained concrete floor mark the entrance to Lipolani (left). Phaleanopsis orchids (top left) and the firecracker-red Pachystachys (top right) add color to the quiet garden, which is an extension of the living room (above).

◆◆◆◆◆◆◆◆◆◆◆◆◆◆◆◆◆◆◆◆◆◆◆◆

Color and Composition

It used to be colorful out here, until my husband became ill," explains Moir. "All of a sudden, the colors became very confining. I decided to remove the color and leave only the green. It became a Zen garden then, a calm and soothing place to be."

In a V-shaped area on the opposite side of the house, an exterior wall, called a *"puka"* wall for its holes, faces the Ko'olau mountains. This major O'ahu mountain range causes the clouds to precipitate and funnels moisture-laden northeasterly trade winds into this valley of waterfalls and dense, tropical rain forest. The wall was built with these details in mind. Concrete blocks were turned on their sides, their hollows becoming air holes so that the epiphytes and bromeliads would be both protected and fed with constantly circulating fresh air.

The living room looks out into this tableau through a five-paneled window seat patterned conceptually after the Japanese screen. Wherever one sits at the window bench, several elements of interest are visible through each glass panel. The Moirs worked as a team, one indoors and the other outside, arranging plants and colors at all heights until the perfect composition presented itself.

"The garden was planted piece by piece and everything was thought out," she explains. "I'd survey from the inside to see what would be best in each panel. We worked to get each form and color at the right height, properly placed for viewing through the window panels." The deep reds in the foliage reflect the reds of the Persian rug indoors and the painting at the end of the living room, uniting indoors and outdoors in one visual and spatial sweep.

"I'm very careful about what I bring into the house. The flowers should be very understated," Moir continues. "I don't feel I have to make a big statement. There are rich colors, but they are not overly demanding. It gives people a peaceful feeling, so that everyone who comes here feels the quiet."

The east side of Lipolani (opposite) is protected from rain and bordered with bromeliads, as is the back garden (left and above) with its twelve varieties of staghorn ferns.

An English garden home in Kula, in earlier times an upcountry ranch house bought from the king of Hawai'i, has an outdoor bathtub (right), a lichen-covered bench (far right), and a veranda smothered in delphiniums and begonias (below). The property also features an ancient cistern that originally provided water for the ranch.

◆◆◆◆◆◆◆◆◆◆◆◆◆◆◆◆◆◆◆◆◆◆

The Night Garden

The rich volcanic soils, the varying microclimates, and the geological diversity in Hawai'i permit a multitude of styles and expressions, from Moir's subdued splendor to flamboyant English gardens and exotic hillsides of native Hawaiian plantings.

Big Island landscape gardener Scott Seymour plans his plantings purposefully, considering when and how the garden will be viewed and appreciated. "Most of my clients have smaller lots, about one-quarter acre to an acre," he explains. "The first things I need to know are their favorite colors, and at what time of the day they'll be using the garden. Many of my clients in Kona are out on the golf course during the day and are only home to watch the sunset, sit on the terrace, and have dinner. This means the only time they can appreciate their gardens is the early morning, or dusk, or at night. For them, I like to plant things that are iridescent in moonlight."

Seymour paints with a palette of fragrances and reflections, inspired by sources as remote as the Mogul rulers of India. "They went out in the moonlight, in a world of night-blooming jasmines, tiares—which bloom in the afternoon and last through the night—and belladonna, which is also very fragrant at night. I think of those flowers and plan my gardens around what will dance in the garden at night."

The large South American philodendron, when it blooms, emits a warm and pungent odor at night from its sensuous, calladium-like flower. In bloom three or four months of the year, it offers fertile ground for Seymour's gardens. Although the night-blooming cereus can pose a problem in maintenance, its ethereal beauty and subtle fragrance make it desirable for areas where it can run rampant.

"Bougainvillea and croton are completely lost at night," he declares. "It's much nicer to go into a home with lush, shiny grays, with mauves, rose, and subtle colors. And off in the corner, if you see a screech of red or a screaming bank of orange, it's appropriate, because it's not blaring into your eyes."

An Acre of the Amazon

On the windward side of O'ahu, where the days are shorter and the sun sinks quickly over the Ko'olau mountains, Hiroshi Tagami and Michael Powell's lush hillside idyll reflects the discerning eye of an artist. The grounds are awash in a tranquil beauty, and colors range from the sultry black of the Negra *ti* plant, obtained in the wilds of Costa Rica, to the variegated hues of the sixty types of anthuriums Tagami has developed and collected. Anthuriums brought back from Machu Picchu and Panama, species collected two hundred miles up the Amazon, and orchids that smell like lemons are among the exotica in Tagami's collection.

He has combed the jungles of Asia and South and Central America and re-created several different ecosystems in his one-acre lot, from the main yard exposed to the sun and wind to the canopied jungle that feels like the Amazon. The temperature drops, and the hot sun on skin cools instantly in the dampness of the dense tropical vegetation that winds down a lush hillside. Every turn brings you face-to-face with rare bamboo, *ti* leaves larger than a person, variegated banana, unearthly anthuriums, and plants that exist nowhere else because they have been hybridized by Tagami.

The Hart, Tagami and Powell Gallery and Gardens combine several media in one coherent aesthetic expression. Carp ponds with lilies flash their colors in the sun. Apples dangle from laden branches, and a bank of day lilies—hundreds of species, developed by Tagami—flaunt their colors every spring. Five gallery spaces house the paintings of Tagami and Michael Powell, as well as antiques, ceramics, hand-turned vessels of native woods, and other fine art works by local artists.

The grounds are a living canvas for Tagami, whose eye for color and design and healthy respect for the wildness of nature are reflected in every vine, tree, flower, shrub, and seedling he has personally planted on the property. His is a garden of tranquillity, with sensitive rhythms that allow the viewer to absorb and rest at intervals. "Of course, to eliminate and simplify is very difficult," he adds. "When you have too many plants, the garden can get too busy. If you don't want it to look garish, you have to constantly simplify. And of course, a garden is never finished." Tagami recently added a rock garden bordering one of the five gallery spaces. Made of volcanic cinders from Hawai'i island, it offers a refreshing, spartan beauty. "Suddenly you're looking at something that's very simple," he says. "The eye has a chance to rest."

A touch of Japan in the Hart, Tagami and Powell Gallery and Gardens in O'ahu (below left). Opposite: A bamboo ladle and lava-rock basin (top left) greet visitors.

On the leeward side of the island, in the blistering sun of Wai'anae, succulents and bougainvillea thrive in the shade provided by a weathered quonset hut (above and left).

Wearing the Garden

The generous rains, caused by the precipitation of the trade winds against the Koʻolaus, make Tagami's a different kind of garden than any that could exist on the dry leeward side of the island. There, Robert Pag-dilao has challenged the elements, and succeeded.

If logic and convention had prevailed in his part of the island, his *maile* vines and *ʻōhiʻa* trees would never have survived. Instead these indigenous plants have thrived, along with ten different types of *ti* plants, bonsai bougainvilleas, breadfruit trees, succulents, fifty orchid plants, and fertile tangerine trees that yield two hundred pounds of fruit a year. The setting? A small yard with a quonset hut.

"I was in a car accident, and for three years, I couldn't work because I lost forty percent of the use of my left arm," Pagdilao recounts. "Friends came and brought plants. I'd say that ninety-five percent of the plants in my yard were given to me. To this day, I remember exactly who gave me each plant."

Unable to work after eighteen years in the shipyard, Pagdilao painstakingly cleared the yard with the use of only his right hand. "I was angry, but the yard made me enjoy life again," he says. "It was the best therapy anyone could have, mentally and physically."

The garden also provided materials for the leis and costumes his wife needed as a dancer in a *hālau hula*. The fluffy *lehua* blossoms from the *ʻōhiʻa* trees, the *plumeria*, and the variegated orchids ensure ongoing adornment for family and friends. "Our yard guarantees that my wife has flowers to wear in her hair every day of the week," says Pagdilao. "The *tiare*, orchids, *lehua*, cattleyas, and dendrobiums—I love to see them in her hair."

A distinctive feature of Hawaiʻi's gardens is not only the way they are designed, planted, grown, and tended, but also the way they are worn. Islanders love to wear their gardens—in leis around their heads, ankles, and necks, behind the ears in dainty clusters, in the sky-high

coifs of colorful Hawaiian aunties who bear in their bouffants and buns the entire floriculture of the Islands. These practices bespeak garden style in Hawaiʻi, a style that is unabashedly, and sometimes mawkishly, in love with the floral kingdom.

The love for plants runs deep because the Hawaiian culture is land-based and inherently spiritual, with values that reach back to the traditional religious life of the ancients. *Palapalai* ferns, *ʻōhiʻa lehua, ʻieʻie,* and *maile* were among the plants placed on the hula altar as an offering to Laka, the patron deity of the dance. Once dedicated, they could not be given to or worn as a lei by another. Even today these plants are held in high esteem, and it is said among the Hawaiian elders that the spicy fragrance of *maile* continues to linger at the sites of ancient *heiau*.

"It's a love story," claims hula teacher and entertainer Kealoha Kalama, who is rarely seen without elaborate floral arrangements in her hair. "You can't separate our love for flowers from our love for the land. There is a Hawaiian song about a special kind of rain that is blown upon the land. It explains how the wind and the rain are like two lovers. When the wind comes and meets the rain, they water the land and bring life to it. The flower, when it blooms from a barren lava field, is the land coming to life, expressing love for us."

The front yard of a home on the North Shore, O'ahu, though battered by the winter winds, sports colorful bougainvillea (left), a row of old Chinese vases (below), and obake anthurium (below left).

A twelve-acre garden estate in Kīlauea, Kaua'i (opposite), has *plumeria* trees, pavilions, a mock orange maze, cannas, and a pool.

Hawai'i's most memorable contemporary homes may be worlds apart in appearance, but they have certain elements in common. One, some aesthetes would say, is a liberation from the confines of good taste. The homes may be aesthetically pleasing and even, yes, tasteful, but they are also free from the demands of convention. Contemporary

homes of high style—Hawai'i style—may be Asian or western in structure, spare in decor or awash in antiques, simple, opinionated, or conspicuously understated. They may be high-rise cocoons creatively inhabited, or oceanfront manors open to the wildness of the elements.

Regardless of its form, in Hawai'i's fabled environment the success of a home can be gauged by the extent to

which one is allowed to live with nature. "**I**t means working with a sense of space, and trying to do what's appropriate," comments Honolulu interior designer

CONTEMPORARY *Style*

A blue hyacinth macaw and two Grand Eclectus parrots flank the "pond," which doubles as a Jacuzzi (above). The living room of the five-bedroom Diamond Head home designed by Albert Groblewski III (right) overlooks the ocean.

Opposite: Gold Thai carvings adorn the front door (left). A view through the mirrored master bathroom (top right); a piano that belonged to Queen Victoria, made in 1870 and formerly displayed in Buckingham Palace (bottom right). The queen's name is on every piece.

Mary Philpotts McGrath. "We should take advantage of what's unique about Hawai'i. The use of materials is different, and we have a great deal of freedom because we don't have to deal with insulation and weather changes."

The elements that prevail in a successful contemporary home are a sensitivity to the climate, wide eaves for rainstorms, large window and door apertures, shade areas, gardens, and the penetration of the interior into the exterior—what McGrath aptly calls "a quality that makes it hard to find the door." Indeed, in a well-designed Island home, one can move seamlessly from one room to the next, one level to another, and from the indoors to the outdoors, without appearing to cross a threshold. When a view doesn't exist, one attempts to create a view, or the illusion of one. Bountiful plants on an urban *lānai*, well-placed greenery in a viewless cocoon, and an indoor-outdoor spatial sweep reflect the fluidity and resourcefulness of style. "There are broad views and intimate views, and we can achieve them in Hawai'i easily because we don't have to insulate, and because we depend so much on the natural air flow," continues McGrath.

Binding these elements are the judiciously selected materials for windows, walls, and floors. Minimalist window coverings, such as sliding shutters and sunshades, are appropriately functional rather than decorative, opening the oceanfront *lānai* to the balmy sea breeze or protecting it from the morning sun. Floor and wall finishings that are cool to the touch—such as stone, slate, terrazzo, wood, tile, and concrete—may be aesthetic decisions, but are, foremost, design tools and tactile elements that complement the warmth of the climate.

Designed by a woman architect and built in 1931, the McGraths' sprawling home (below and opposite) is surrounded by lush gardens. The house incorporates Mediterranean, Chinese, and Hawaiian influences—plus a meticulously restored 1960 Thunderbird.

The McGraths' Island eclectic Nu'uanu home contains a round China Trade table (above), a carved wood table from the Royal Hawaiian Hotel (far left), and a Maori chest by George Moody (left).

Sugar Plantation Koloa Kauai 1841

Walls and thresholds are unobtrusive in this sleek Diamond
Head manse designed by Vladimir
Ossipoff, built for outdoor living,
even at night (above left). Details
of a life in the sun (above) hang
on the bathroom wall.

An Easygoing Gallery

Opposite: Floors of polished *koa* and stained concrete, trompe l'oeil, and carved wooden Chinese panels in the living room make this 1939 Diamond Head home a visual feast.

The red brick patio (top) was created for an outdoor lifestyle; the stately high-pitched roofline (above) is a Hawaiian signature.

As for how the home is inhabited, how objects are collected and used, that is style in action, too. Fueled by their passion and commitment, collectors such as Laila Twigg-Smith have practical and aesthetic concerns that only begin with space.

Given the choice, Twigg-Smith would have preferred a less humid climate for her nine-hundred-piece art collection. "But should we be punished because we happen to live in Hawai'i?" she ponders, surveying the world-class collection of contemporary art that dominates her Diamond Head home. Rather than compromise on the installation of the art, the Twigg-Smiths choose to display it outdoors, indoors, anywhere that aesthetically pleases them, salt air and rain be damned. "We have to be a little bit cavalier if we're going to live here," she asserts. "There's no question the works are affected by the elements, but we feel this is the way they are meant to be enjoyed."

The house has been renovated three times to accommodate the collection, which grows daily, spilling purposefully out into the patio and outdoor areas and uniting the separate spaces according to how the works are placed. Pieces move in and out—on loan, in changing displays, under ever-changing weather conditions. Some rooms are temperature- and moisture-controlled. The sculptures are waxed every three months and the paintings are rotated regularly, and overall, a good measure of vigilance and maintenance is required.

"It would be much more difficult to live with all these things if we couldn't move in and out," Twigg-Smith admits. "The movement and rhythm of the house are very important." The four-bedroom home was designed by Bertram Goodhue (who also designed the Honolulu Academy of Arts). Its high-pitched roofline and open-air patio and living-room areas epitomize Hawai'i-style architecture, but are not what one notices immediately. It's the pieces—a serious

151

collection balanced with brilliant flashes of humor—that dominate: the spears of primary colors in Don King's stained-wood dining chairs, the Deborah Butterfield discarded-metal horse, the Roy De Forest painted wood sculpture, John Buck's *El Diablo*. The Dale Chihuly glass adds a strong stroke of elegance to the open-air living room, and the Joel Otterson tea cart and Gerald Heffernon self-portrait express wit and whimsy in far corners. The works by Georgia O'Keeffe, Cy Twombly, Frank Stella, David Hockney, H. C. Westermann, Wayne Thiebaud, Richard Diebenkorn, Robert Mapplethorpe, and Billy Al Bengston are serious yet unpretentiously placed.

The polished *'ōhi'a* and *koa* wood floors have been bleached to add light, which streams in generously from all sides of the living room and reflects off the white walls. The patio overlooks the Waikīkī skyline, and the fluid open space creates indistinct boundaries between outdoor and indoor areas. Taking full advantage of the Island climate and the gentle beauty of the Diamond Head setting, the works are displayed in staggering yet orderly profusion.

In surprising corners nestle the hands, hearts, lady head vases, teapots, masks, Royal Copenhagen Christmas plates, and beer bottles that have been collected, documented, and recorded with a passion. "All of these things on the walls are documented by size, country, state, type, down to the smallest detail," Twigg-Smith continues, pointing to the beer bottle collection of her husband, Thurston. "We must have forty Heineken bottles, and every one is different."

The Twigg-Smiths' most ambitious installation to date is the 201 television sets of Nam Jun Paik's *Fin de Siècle*, which required a crew of nine, a week of time, special fans, an entire wall of shelving, and a separate infrastructure for display.

"You have all these works, and you have only so much wall. It's so delicate," Twigg-Smith reflects. "There are very, very few things that stay. Works constantly go out on loan to museums, or go on the road. The pieces are in constant movement. The environment is kinetic, so it can be confusing. Installation is so important, because you don't want to be confused, and displaying the work is like putting your personality out for others to see."

A walk through the *ʻōhiʻa*-and-*koa*-floored living room brings the visitor an encounter with Roy de Forest's painted wood sculpture (above) and Deborah Butterfield's discarded-metal horse (left).

Opposite: Looking like a mural, the Waikīkī skyline looms beyond the bronze sculpture by Charles Arnoldi and copper frieze by Mark Bulwinkle (top); a bronze by Robert Arneson with a glass sculpture by Howard Ben Tré (bottom).

153

Contemporary Hawaiian design elements from the 1930s and a large poolside Singapore *plumeria* tree distinguish this 'Aina Haina retreat (above and above right). The owner added a second floor and rebuilt the low-pitched wooden country house so all rooms open to the outdoors.

Opposite: Antiques include the "Four Accomplishments" Chinese screen (top left), an eighteenth-century Rimpa School screen in the bedroom (center left), an Edo-period Enma (judge of hell) on a Ming-dynasy painting table (bottom left), and a late-nineteenth-century Chinese daybed fronting one of two pianos in the house (far right).

A Patchwork House

The ephemeral nature of environments requires a certain detachment. In 'Āina Haina, Honolulu, John Komu took a country home built after World War II and rebuilt it into a contemporary Hawaiian-style dwelling where every room on the main floor opens out into the yard. Because building supplies were scarce when the home was originally built, scavenged wood, wood of all types and colors, was used. "When we tore open the ceiling and looked at the roof," Komu explains, "we found that a couple barn doors were used to build it."

The house appears, like a mirage, from a well-hidden suburban corner. Light streams in to illuminate a collection of Asian antiques acquired over more than twenty-five years. "I wanted the feeling of an old *kama'āina* home with full access to the outdoors," Komu notes. "I had all these pieces, so the house was constructed for them as well." A clean, serene aesthetic is in full expression here, with seventeenth-century Ming furniture, Edo- period Japanese screens, antique lacquer from Gump's, and the discreet placement of two baby grand pianos, a harpsichord, and a Madge Tennent original over the fireplace. Bathed in natural light, the pieces and architecture unite harmoniously, achieving Komu's goal of tranquillity, peace, and elegance.

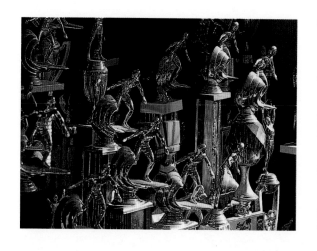

There are homes for people, and homes for collections. Because the collections follow the people, most shelters accommodate both. **B**ut there are rooms that reveal a life with far more intimacy than a collection alone can convey. The story is in the way the dust has collected on the medals, or the way the newspaper article has torn and yellowed. The rusty inscription on a pocketknife may speak volumes about its keeper, and so can the one empty dowel on the hat rack of worn fedoras. Use and time have a way of achieving their own value, fathomable only to the collector. Linger awhile among the shelves of memorabilia, the newly polished heirlooms, the treasured calabashes with their nicks and scratches. Stories unfold around them. **T**he rows of horse figurines, three gener-

ations of muddy boots in a corner, the aerie plastered with pictures—life leaves its codes in unexpected places.

ROOMS THAT TELL A *Story*

◆◆◆◆◆◆◆◆◆◆◆◆◆◆◆◆◆◆◆◆◆◆

The Unwitting Collector

Few people are prepared for the profusion of objects that cover the walls, dangle from the ceilings, line the shelves, and spill out of scrapbooks in the Maui home of David and Violet Cup Choy, who live happily in the shadow of their mementos. Although the shiny silver bomb casings doubling as fence posts outside should be a signal that surprises lurk within, guests still gasp when the front door opens. A glittering canopy of mobiles and oceans of Walt Disney figurines (including two sets of Snow White and the Seven Dwarfs), neon signs, origami figures, lamps (one made from a hand-crank phonograph), antique phones and cash registers, wooden bowls and statues, mugs, plastic fruit, clocks, ashtrays, balloons, plates, maps, cookie jars, toys, fishing balls, calendars, posters, and salt and pepper shakers by the hundreds line every square inch of wall and ceiling space in the couple's four-bedroom home. "We remember who gave us each thing," David Cup Choy declares simply.

"I was a nurse," explains seventy-nine-year-old Violet Cup Choy. "I did quite a bit of nursing without being paid, because people needed care and couldn't afford a nurse. So the patients gave me these things. I never threw anything away. I had to put each thing up, so when the people came to visit, they'd see their gifts and know I appreciate them."

Her husband proudly displays a sixty-five-year-old teddy bear, the first stuffed animal he gave her in the first days of their friendship. They have been married fifty-four years. "We were coming home from the county fair and the man said to me, 'Come and try your luck,'" he recounts. "I put a dollar down and spun the wheel, ten cents at a time, for the lucky number that won this bear."

Their gray home with pink and green trim has been expanded and renovated since his father first lived there at the turn of the century, and since David himself was born there in 1910. There are poems left by

homeless hippies who were given shelter in the spare room; souvenirs and letters from children, now grown up, who were taken in, fed, and clothed; accounts of their driving lost visitors around the island and passersby sheltered there during the war. Once, when a woman asked them to care for her baby while she went to O'ahu to get married, they did—for two and a half years. Every nook and cranny in the home, and the hundreds of thousands of photographs spilling out of albums and scrapbooks, harbor memories of a long life lived in kindness.

"I have a lot of amazing stories," says David Cup Choy of Makawao, Maui, whose kitchen and patio (opposite and above) tell half of them. Some of the hundreds of cookie jars, salt and pepper shakers, and other kitchen paraphernalia in the family (right), and a cornerful of mementos from Reno (far right).

Cecil's Beauty Salon in Chinatown, Honolulu, is a world of parrots and gilded saints. Owner Guss Esposo, a native Filipino and a Catholic, dresses the figurines of the patron saints with costumes he makes himself. All the figurines are custom-made, and, according to the owner, the devotional decor is indeed calming to some of his customers.

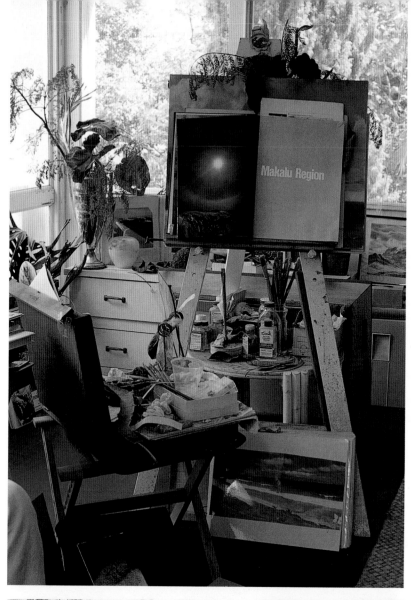

In upcountry Maui, a different kind of room bespeaks a different passion. The second-floor, light-filled artist's studio is chockablock with open books, pages torn, pictures mounted, and yellowed articles, photographs, and posters scattered and displayed spiritedly. Coffee-table books and periodicals have relinquished their glossy pages of mountain views, snowcapped crests, distant gorges, the Alps, Andes, Himalayas, Rockies—the world's inventory of peaks—for the ongoing perusal of the artist, who paints (what else?) mountains.

161

It could be a tarp shelter, a hammock on the beach, a sagging stable patched with Bondo and rescued from the wrecker's ball. It could be the overgrown ruins of a sugar mill, restored and reborn as a mountainside idyll for an artist. Bags of concrete, a few cans of paint,

recycled wooden water tanks, old glass windows from a plantation house—there's no mystery to the materials.

The vagabond's house is just one more way the free-spirited can live comfortably, using modest means to build castles in the sky. It was twelve years ago that Maui artist Reems Mitchell discovered the ruins of the Makee sugar mill on an evening stroll in 'Ulupalakua. In a year and a half it was cleared, but the work hadn't even begun. "There was an old playhouse I found elsewhere," he recalls. "I took the ceiling out, rearranged it, and hauled it here. It sat like a pretzel for two to three years." Eventually he installed windows from an old plantation house. Salt-bleached doors from the beach, recycled wood from water tanks, dismantled garages, troughs from the 'Ulupalakua Ranch, and vestiges of other old buildings became his materials. A tent was his home while he built.

THE *Vagabond's* HOUSE

"Finally, I jacked up the house, stuccoed it, and made it look old," he recounts with pride. "I wanted it to look like stone."

You can still see the ocean (right) from the old Makee sugar mill (opposite), Maui artist Reems Mitchell's monument to resourcefulness.

Repeated experiments with concrete led him to a black, fungus-like effect that he used triumphantly as a finishing in strategic corners.

The old, rusty boiler from the sugar mill still stands behind the house like a sculpture, a reminder of the days when the plantation hummed with its rose gardens, sugar, and cattle operations. The concrete trough where the sugarcane juice flowed is now festooned with impatiens, next to a square pond that held the freshly squeezed juice before it was routed to the cookers. The corrugated iron roofs are rusty—unobtrusive in this setting, blending with the high concrete mill tower that has been preserved as a part of the house structure.

The old playhouse has become Mitchell's bedroom, festive and airy with light streaming in through its recycled plantation-house windows. Like all parts of this Hobbit-like complex, the main house invites lingering. The crossbeams in the ceiling came from sturdy old water tanks, which also provided the thick wooden louvers—each individually installed—used in the doors and floors of the house.

Found materials are the boon of creative builders, particularly in Hawai'i, where one can live comfortably in the most modest and basic of shelters. More than a few homeowners have used pineapple pallets, old doors, scrap wood, hand-logged pillars, and other found objects to give new life to old buildings that have remained their homes for years.

One Nu'uanu, O'ahu, couple used a hefty dose of Bondo and ingenuity to prove the naysayers wrong. "Three contractors told us to torch it," said the resident, an artist. "Instead, we plugged up the holes with Bondo. The house was full of rot and had to be hoisted up." Once a stable, a laborers' camp, and a men's dormitory, the shack that received a reprieve is now a paragon of creativity. The opalescence of rare glass shoots streams of light across the kitchen, and views from the second-floor living space look out into palatial gardens. Haitian hangings, a tile entrance, camouflage-painted walls, and offbeat collections of objects from the beach make this a home to remember.

Wood from old water tanks, doors found on the beach, old plantation-house windows, and cement made to look like fungus were among Mitchell's materials. The original stack from the Makee sugar mill is still visible (far left).

Opposite: Mitchell's painting of his mother (above center); the bedroom, living room, and guest room; and kitchen cabinets made from old doors.

This wooden home in Ha'ikū, Maui (far left, above), was overgrown with cane grass when its owner moved in twenty years ago. Today the complex includes two homes, a hot tub, chicken coops, lush gardens, and native plants such as *ti*, ginger, *kukui*, and *laua'e* ferns.

Fabric panels secured by bamboo rods do wonders for the ceiling, and floral curtains have replaced the pretty dresses that occasionally adorn the front window (above).

The shade of the overhanging trees blocks much of the available light, so the owner of the wooden house used tropical paint colors to brighten the kitchen (far left, below; and left, above and below).

169

Handmade tiles at the entrance, a handmade mosaic pillar, and heliconias picked from the garden enliven this Nuʻuanu Valley home (above). An eclectic glass collection brightens the kitchen (right), and the living room and bedroom (opposite) are infused with light.

The kitchen-without-walls is detached from this octagonal house (above and left) at a solar-operated farm in Pa'auilo, Hawai'i island. The fruit and flowers are from the garden.

Opposite: Vagabonds in Hawai'i, where the elements are kinder than most other places, can live in trees, under temporary tarp shelters, or on the beach.

Living on the Volcano

Ironically, even vagabonds' homes like Reems Mitchell's are no more or less transient than others, for Hawai'i's dynamic environment dares us to subscribe to the illusion of permanence. With all of the bolsters, balustrades, supports, and securities built into our notions of the home, there remains a built-in impermanence to Hawai'i's style of living. Hawai'i's openness to the elements is a comfort and a privilege, but it is also a vulnerability. "Whether it's through inundation from the inlands or consumption by the sea, or even through an active lava flow, if you're a cognizant person living in a dynamic environment like Hawai'i, you recognize the transient nature of your abode," reflects Big Island *kama'āina* Hannah Springer.

"No matter how carefully we *mālama* [take care], it does us well to recognize the transient nature of things. Nearly two centuries ago, the eruption of Hualālai (on the Big Island) consumed breadfruit groves and fishponds in Kekaha; recently, the town of Kalapana was covered with lava. If we choose to live on an active volcano, it's wise to adopt a world view that incorporates the elements in all forms—not only as sustaining, but as consuming. . . ."

Indeed, in the chants of Hawai'i the earth trembles, trees groan, and curtains of fire become garments of Pele. "And thou, O Pele, then ate of thy land," says Nathaniel B. Emerson's *Pele and Hiiaka*, "consuming the groves of 'ōhi'a, and Lele'iwi's palms by the sea."

No wonder Don Blanding, in his poem "The Vagabond's House," built the home of his dreams with words. It was this poem that inspired Reems Mitchell while he built his Eden out of the ruins of the old Makee sugar mill:

> *And the thought will strike with a swift sharp pain*
> *That I probably never will build again*
> *This house that I'll have in some far day.*
> *Well . . . it's just a dream house anyway.*

In the end the elements prevail, as with these homes in Kalapana, Hawai'i island, a village wiped out by lava in 1990 by the forces of the volcano goddess, Pele.

Glossary

'āina the land.

akamai smart, clever, wise.

ali'i chief, king, queen; Hawaiian royalty.

aloha hello, good-bye, love, kindness, regards.

'auana modern hula.

'awapuhi wild ginger.

Diamond Head in Honolulu, an easterly direction, or toward Diamond Head.

'ewa in Honolulu, in a westerly direction, or toward 'Ewa.

hala pandanus, or screw pine, whose dried leaves are woven into *lauhala* mats and accessories, and whose fruit are sewn into leis.

hālau a Hawaiian longhouse where hula and other Hawaiian arts are taught; a school.

hale house.

hale kuku house for beating kapa.

haole Caucasian.

hapa-haole half-haole, or half-Caucasian.

hau a lowland tree with heart-shaped leaves and wood used in the outriggers of canoes. It also has medicinal uses, and its bast was used in rope and sandals.

hau'oli glad, happy, joyful.

heiau pre-Christian place of worship.

hikie'e a large Hawaiian couch.

holoholo a pleasant excursion or outing.

hula Hawaiian dance.

imu underground oven of heated lava rocks.

ipu gourd, usually used to carry water or food, or as an instrument in hula.

kahiko ancient hula; old.

kāhili feather standard, a symbol of royalty.

kahuna priest or minister; expert in any profession.

kai sea, ocean.

kama'āina old-timer; or native, local, or longtime resident.

kamani a large hardwood tree used to make calabashes.

kāne man.

kapa Hawaiian bark cloth, often called *tapa*.

kapakahi crooked, lopsided, showing favoritism.

kapu taboo, forbidden.

keiki child.

kiawe the algaroba tree, or mesquite.

kīhei blanket or shawl.

koa also called Acacia *koa*; a native forest tree whose wood is popularly in use in furniture and bowls.

kōkua help, cooperation, assistance.

kolohe naughty, mischievous.

kou a tree of Polynesian origin whose wood was used by the early Hawaiians for dishes and calabashes.

kukui candlenut tree.

kuleana property, responsibility, jurisdiction; a small piece of property; land division.

kumu teacher, model, guide; beginning, source.

kupuna grandparent, real or adopted; ancestor; a respected elder.

lānai veranda, porch, balcony.

lauhala pandanus leaf.

lehua the fluffy flower, usually red, of the *'ōhi'a* tree; may be yellow, various shades of red, or, in extremely rare cases, white.

leina place where spirits leap into the nether world; leap of the souls; to spring or leap.

liliko'ī passion fruit.

limu seaweed.

lua bathroom.

lū'au Hawaiian feast.

mahalo thank you.

maika'i good, excellent, fine; handsome or beautiful.

maile an anise-scented native shrub with leaves used in leis, decorations, and as traditional offerings to Laka, goddess of the hula.

makai toward the ocean.

mālama to care for, preserve; custodian or caretaker.

malihini newcomer, tourist, visitor.

mana spiritual power or presence.

mana'o opinion, knowledge, thoughts and ideas.

mauka toward the mountains.

mele a song or chant that is performed.

milo a popular shade tree among early Hawaiians; a wood used in bowls and calabashes.

nani splendor, glory, beauty; beautiful; how much, how.

nui great; important; large or big.

'ohana family.

'ōhi'a a native Hawaiian tree with fluffy flowers (called *lehua* blossoms) and strong wood often used for posts.

'ōlapa dancer; a dance accompanied by chanting and drumming on a gourd drum; several native species and varieties of forest trees.

oli Hawaiian chant that is not danced to.

ono delicious; *wahoo* (a popular game fish).

'opihi limpet.

pali cliff.

paniolo Hawaiian cowboy.

pau finished.

pehea 'oe How are you?

pōhaku stone, rock.

poi Hawaiian staple, a paste made of cooked *taro*.

puka hole, door, gate.

pūne'e movable couch.

pupu appetizer.

tutu grandmother.

'umeke wooden bowls used to store food.

wahine woman.

wikiwiki quick, hurry, soon.

Bibliography

Armstrong, R. Warwick, editor and project director. *Atlas of Hawaii*. Honolulu: University of Hawaii Press, 1983.

Beechert, Ed. *Working in Hawaii: A Labor History*. Honolulu: University Press of Hawaii, 1985.

Bird, Isabella. *Six Months in the Sandwich Islands*. Rutland, VT: Charles E. Tuttle Co., Inc., 1974.

Blanding, Don. *Vagabond's House*. New York: Dodd, Mead & Company, 1928.

Buck, Peter. *Arts and Crafts of Hawaii*. Honolulu: Bishop Museum Press, 1957.

Char, Tin-Yuke. *The Sandalwood Mountains*. Honolulu: University Press of Hawaii, 1975.

Elbert, Samuel H., Mary Kawena Pukui, and Esther T. Mookini. *Place Names of Hawaii*. Honolulu: University Press of Hawaii, 1974.

Emerson, Nathaniel B. *Pele and Hi-iaka: A Myth from Hawaii*. Rutland, VT: Charles E. Tuttle Co., Inc., 1978.

Fuchs, Lawrence. *Hawaii Pono*. New York: Harcourt Brace Jovanovich, 1961.

Hawaii Insight Guides. Hong Kong: Apa Productions, 1980.

Hawaii Sugar News. Honolulu. October 1951.

Hawaiian Planters' Record. Honolulu. No 4, April 1920; No. 6, June 1920; Vol. XXV, No. 2, August 1921; Vol. XXX, No. 1, January 1926.

Honolulu Advertiser. Honolulu. September 8, 1947.

I'i, John Papa. *Fragments of Hawaiian History*. Honolulu:, Bishop Museum Press, 1959.

Jenkins, Irving. *Hawaiian Furniture and Hawaii's Cabinetmakers*. Honolulu: Editions Limited, 1983.

Kaaihue, Marmie, editor. *Songs of Helen Desha Beamer*. Honolulu: A. K. Kawananakoa Foundation, 1991.

Kamakau, Samuel. *The Works of the People of Old (Na Hana a ka Po'e Kahiko)*. Honolulu: Bishop Museum Press, 1976.

Kanahele, George. *Kū Kanaka*. Honolulu: University of Hawaii Press, 1986.

Kingston, Maxine Hong. *China Men*. New York: Alfred A. Knopf, 1980.

Krauss, Bob, with W. P. Alexander. *Grove Farm Plantation*. Palo Alto, CA: Pacific Books, 1984.

Malo, David. *Hawaiian Antiquities*. Honolulu: Bishop Museum Press, 1951.

Martin, Lynn, editor and project director. *Nā Paniolo o Hawai'i*. Honolulu Academy of Arts, 1987.

McAlester, Virginia and Lee. *A Field Guide to American Houses*. New York: Alfred A. Knopf, 1984.

Pukui, Mary Kawena, and Samuel H. Elbert. *Hawaiian Dictionary*. Honolulu: University of Hawaii Press, 1971.

Takaki, Ronald. *Pau Hana*. Honolulu: University of Hawaii Press, 1984.

Timmons, Grady. *Waikiki Beachboy*. Honolulu: Editions Limited, 1989.

Von Tempski, Armine. *Born in Paradise*, 1940. Woodbridge, CT: Ox Bow Press, 1985 (reprint).

Acknowledgments

"'A'ohe hana nui ke alu 'ia!"

"No task is too big when done together by all."

—Mary Kawena Pukui

It was indeed a big task, but many opened their hearts and homes so this book could be realized.

There are few things more personal than homes. Those who lifted the curtains of privacy for this book exhibited a grace and generosity that are rare. My sincere gratitude to all who invited us into their homes, who guided us with suggestions or ideas, and who gave time, encouragement, and expertise to the completion of this project.

This book is the brainchild of my agents, Katharine Sands and Sarah Jane Freymann, two indefatigable New Yorkers who proved that you don't have to live in Hawai'i to see and appreciate the nuances of its style. To Joan Tapper of *Islands* magazine, thank you for bringing us together.

I will always be thankful to Jane von Mehren, my friend and former editor, for her unflagging support throughout our rich and abiding association. At Crown I would like to thank Mark McCauslin, Joy Sikorsky, Mercedes Everett, Lauren Dong, and especially Ken Sansone for his masterful design. Etya Pinker was invaluable in her attention to the myriad details of this years-long collaboration. No one worked more closely on this book with me than my editor at Crown, Erica Marcus. To her I owe an enormous debt of gratitude for ushering this book through to completion with the consummate professionalism, good judgment, and discernment for which she is known. I am very fortunate to have had the opportunity to work with such a team.

I can never adequately thank Paul Theroux—not only a generous contributor to this book but also a kind friend and brilliant observer, whose insights on Hawai'i have made living here a lot more fun. A special *mahalo* also to Sheila Donnelly, herself an arbiter of style, for her generous contributions of time, ideas, and resources—and most of all for her spirited friendship and encouragement throughout the years. There are numerous others who contributed generously in everything from compiling the shot list to finding resources to reminiscing and "talking story." Listed alphabetically, they are: Carol Austin, Jody Baldwin, Jackie Blackshear, Roy Blackshear, Tom Boda, Lindy Boyes, Mary Cade, Barbara Campbell, Richard Chamberlain, Marsha Erickson, Kaui Goring, Dr. Brysson Greenwell, Gwen Herrington, Marmie Kaaihue, Millie Kaiserman, Val Kim, Val Knudsen, Ann Marsteller, Micah Miller, Linda O'Connor and her Clair de Lune Collection, Virgo Paynter, Martin Rabbett, Franco Salmoiraghi, Jan Selland, Bill Souza, Grady Timmons, Alice Tracy, Laila and Thurston Twigg-Smith, Yakzan Valdez, and Susan Yim.

Many thanks to all those who assisted photographer Linny Morris Cunningham: Bill and Jane Morris, Sammy and Auwe Morris, Elizabeth M. Myers, Debbie Brown, Geoffrey Bourne, Brian and Caverly Kennelly, and Mark Cunningham.

For her wisdom and guidance and friendship, and for her enormous contribution to the spirit and content of this book, *mahalo nui loa* to Hannah Springer. Special thanks also go to Creighton and Annette Fujii, my Kaua'i team and headquarters for all projects. For their inspiration, encouragement, and confidence, I thank Joan and Linc Diamant in New York. Very special acknowledgment goes to my New York family, Anne and Lloyd Moss, for their unending generosity. They have contributed enormously to my personal and professional life from long before the doors of publishing were open to me. And to my *kupuna*, Nana Veary, *me ke aloha pau 'ole.*

Finally, I bow deeply to my father, Dr. Kenneth Fujii. His unconditional love sustains my every endeavor.

Index

ina Haina, 154
Alaka'i Swamp, 119
Alexanader and Baldwin building, 24, 57
"aloha stones," as decor, 127
Aluli, Irmgard Farden, 41, 43

Bailey, Roselle, 119, 121–122
Baldwin, Jody, 113–114
Beamer, Helen Desha, 40–41, 50
Beechert, Ed, 64, 66
Bernice Pauahi Bishop Museum, 26, 28
Big Island, *see* Hawai'i
Bird, Isabella, 122
Blackshear, Jackie, 48, 50
Blackshear, Roy Shipman, 48, 50
Blanding, Don, 174
Born in Paradise (von Tempski), 93
Brown, DeSoto, 26, 30
Brown, Francis I'i, 40
Buckley, Brent, 92
Buddhist temple, 27

Carter, A. W., 80
Carvalho, Josephine, 104
Castle and Cooke, 68
C. Brewer building, 28
Cecil's Beauty Salon, 160
ceremonies, housewarming, 14, 18, 21
chants and songs, 36, 40–41, 73, 122, 123
Circle-J Ranch, 82
collectibles, as decor, 35, 39, 43, 47, 50, 51, 62, 65, 73, 125, 127, 144–145, 148–153, 154, 157–161, 164, 170
contemporary style, 143–155
Cook, Captain James, 21, 59
Coryell, Roger, 127
cowboys, *see* paniolo
Cup Choy, David, 158–159
Cup Choy, Violet, 158–159

Danford home, 122–23
Davis, Charles K. L., 40, 50
Davis, Louis, 130
Diamond Head, 27, 106, 144, 151–153
Dickey, Charles William, 24, 26, 28, 46–47, 57, 59
diversity:
  of climate, 12
  of cultures, 12, 14, 26, 34, 59, 67, 68, 80, 82, 85
  geographical, 12
  geological, 135

Elbert, Samuel H., 36
Emerson, Nathaniel B., 174
Emma, Queen of Hawai'i, 119
Erickson, Marsha, 120, 123
Esposo, Guss, 160
'Ewa Plantation, 64, 67, 68

Faye, Mike, 57, 59, 64, 66, 67
flowers, wearing of, 93, 129, 139
found materials, 154, 163, 164

Gardens, 68, 114, 120, 123, 129–141, 146, 172
Goodhue, Bertram, 151
Goodwin, William, 123
Greenwell, Brysson, 82–83, 84–86, 90, 92
Groblewski, Albert, III, 144

Hā'ena, 48, 50
Hā'ikū 127, 169
Haleakalā, 41, 120, 127
Haleakalā Ranch, 93
Halekulani Hotel, 30
Halemanu, 114
Hāmākua, 27, 56, 69
Hanalei, 43–46, 65
Hart, Tagami and Powell Gallery and Gardens, 136–137
Hawai'i (Big Island), 12–13, 19, 20, 21, 22, 27, 28, 41, 48, 50, 56, 57, 66, 69, 70, 76, 79, 80, 81, 83–87, 90, 92, 96, 108, 114, 117, 127, 129, 135, 136, 172, 174–175
Hawaiian Sugar Planters Association (HSPA), 64, 66
Hawaiian Telephone Co. building, 28
Hilo, 28, 66
Hōlualoa, 56, 120, 125
Honolulu, 13, 21, 24, 26, 28, 57, 154, 160
houses:
  beach, *see* makai
  board-and-batten, 90–91
  grass, 21, 26, 123
  mountain, *see* mauka
  octagonal, 172
  ranch, *see* paniolo
  stone, 59
  surfers', 104–105, 106
  wooden, 21, 56, 118, 169
Hualālai, 41, 174
Hu'ehu'e Ranch, 34, 81
hula, 48, 50, 93, 119, 139
Hulihe'e Palace, 20
Hulme, Kathryn, 119

Indigenous materials, 14, 17, 19, 20, 24, 26, 57, 59, 146
  coral, 20, 21
  as decor, 28, 30, 88
  rattan, 26, 30, 31
  rock, 58
  stone, 28, 36, 118
  see also koa; lava; wood
indoor-outdoor design, 26, 151, 152–153, 172
indoor-outdoor lifestyle, 14, 17–18, 21, 48, 104, 129, 130, 146
Iolani Palace, 24
irrigation ditches, 129
islands:
  creation of, 10
  living on, 8–12
Ives, Bert, 103

Johnson, Jeff, 106

Ka'ahumanu, Queen of Hawai'i, 48
Kāhala, 96, 100
Kahiwawai, 96
Kaho'ohalahala, Sol, 73
Kahuā Ranch, 81, 83–87
Kailua-Kona, 21
Kalahikiola Church, 21
Kalākaua, David, King of Hawai'i, 24, 50, 56
Kalama, Kealoha, 139
Kalapana, 12–13, 174–175
kama'āina, 12, 14, 32–53, 96, 114, 154
Kamakau, Samuel, 18
Kamehameha I (the Great), King of Hawai'i, 34, 48, 56, 80
Kamehameha III, King of Hawai'i, 80
Kamehameha IV, King of Hawai'i, 119
Kaohi, Aletha, 120, 121
Kaua'i, 22, 24, 43–46, 57–58, 59, 65, 69, 114, 118, 119, 120, 122, 140
Kauikeōlani, 43–46
Kawaiaha'o Church, 20, 21
Kawanui, 88–91
Kealakekua, 96
Kealakekua Bay, 101
Kealakekua Ranch, Ltd., 83
Kelley, Roy C., 26, 30
Kīkīla, 48
Kīlauea, 69, 140
Kīlauea Plantation, 58–59, 60–63
Kimura, Yutaka, 80, 93
Kipikane, Rachel, 80
Knudsen, Valdemar, 114, 119
koa, 17, 30, 31, 35, 38, 39, 47, 76, 80, 85, 86, 88–89, 103, 108, 117, 151, 152, 153
Kohala, 41, 81, 86
Kohala Nui Farms, 76
Kōke'e, 13, 114, 118, 119, 120, 121, 122–123, 125

Koke'e Museum, 120

Kōloa, 114

Kōloa Plantation, 24, 59

Komu, John, 154

Kona, 81, 82

Kona Hotel, 120

Ko'olau mountains, 27, 132, 136, 139

Kukuihaele, 57

Kukui'ohiwai, 35

Kula, 13, 81, 114, 115, 127, 134

Kumuhonua, 33

Lana'i, 68, 73

lanais, 21, 26, 30, 52, 57, 146

land:
    dividing of, 96
    love of, 14
    ownership of, 13, 57
    value of, 92

Lanikai, 106, 108

Larsen, L. David, 59

lava, 12, 51
    as building material, 17, 19, 20, 21, 22, 28, 57, 88, 90–91
    as decor, 136
    as destructive force, 12–13
    homes built on, 13, 41, 43, 174
    houses destroyed by, 174–175

lava fields, 129, 139

leeward, 96, 138

Leineweber, Spencer, 45, 55

Lili'uokalani, Queen of Hawai'i, 24, 50

Lipolani, 130–133, 135

McGrath, Mary Philpotts, 143, 146, 148–149

Mahealani Ranch, 88–93

makai, 12, 95–111, 114

Makawao, 93

Makee sugar mill, 163–168, 174

Makiki, 28

Mānā Hale, 86

Mason, Glenn, 14, 21, 24, 26

Maui, 28, 41, 46–47, 81, 93, 103, 114,

115, 125, 127, 158–159, 161, 169

mauka, 12, 13, 96, 113–127

Mauna Kea, 41, 80, 127

Mauna Loa, 41, 83

Maunalua Bay, 106

Miloli'i, 19

missionaries, 12, 21, 22, 43, 48, 50

Mission Houses Museum, 20, 21

Mitchell, Reems, 163–168, 174

Moir, Goodale, 130, 132

Moir, May, 130, 132

Moku'aikaua Church, 20

Mokulua Islands, 108

Mookini, Esther T., 36

mountain house, *see mauka*

Mount Wai'ale'ale, 119

Nene, 48, 50, 51

Nobriga, Barbara, 88–91

Nobriga, Edwin, 88–91

North Kohala, 77, 84

North Kona, 88–91

North Shore, 100, 104–105, 106, 111, 140

Nu'uanu, 30, 52, 117, 148, 164

Nu'uanu Valley, 27, 56, 129–130, 170

O'ahu, 27, 30, 31, 36–39, 52, 56, 64, 92, 96, 100, 104, 106, 108, 111, 132, 136, 140, 164

ocean, 95–111, 174

Olinda, 46–47

Over, Don, 111

Over, Josie, 111

Pa'auilo, 172

Pagdilao, Robert "Puggy," 64, 67, 68, 139

paniolo, 75–93, 114, 134

Papakōlea Moanalua, 36–39

Parker, Hilary, 127

Parker, John Palmer, 80, 81, 86

Parker Ranch, 79, 80–81, 92

Pele, 12, 13, 34, 50, 114, 119, 174–175

Pele and Hiiake (Emerson), 174

Place Names of Hawaii (Elbert), 36

plantation managers' homes, 55, 57, 58, 59, 60–63, 66

plantations, 12, 14, 21, 22, 24, 43, 55–74, 82–83, 114, 127, 164

plantation workers' homes, 55, 57, 64, 66–67

Portlock, 96, 106

Powell, Michael, 136–137

Prosper, Kekaulike, 34

puka wall, 132

Pukui, Mary Kawena, 36

Pu'ulehua, 84–86

Pu'uwa'awa'a, 81

Quonset hut, 138

Ranches, *see paniolo*

Ripley, C. B., 52

roofs:
    corrugated metal, 27, 56, 66, 69, 120, 125
    high-pitched (Dickey), 26, 28, 30, 48, 55, 57, 66, 103, 151
    shingled, 125
    slate, 76
    thatched, 19, 21, 59
    tile, 130

Roy, Eliza, 90

Roy, William F., 90

Sanburn, Marta, 96, 106

Seymour, Scott, 135

Sheehan, Patsy, 43, 45, 48

Shipman, Herbert, 48, 50

Silva, Henry, 81

Six Months in the Sandwich Islands (Bird), 122

solar-operated farm, 172

Springer, Hannah Kihalani, 33–34, 174

story-telling rooms, 157–161

surf, 96, 100, 106

surfboards, as decor, 105, 106

Tagami, Hiroshi, 136–137

Theroux, Paul, 8–12

Timmons, Grady, 108

Tomich, Michael, 33

Tracy, Alice, 100

Twigg-Smith, Laila, 151–152

Ulupalakua, 163–164

Vagabonds, 161–175

"Vagabond's House, The" (Blanding), 174

Vancouver, George, 80

verandas, 45, 48, 70, 76–77, 114

Volcano, 13, 114, 120, 125, 127

volcanoes, 12, 13

von Tempski, Armine, 93

von Tempski, Louis, 93

Wai'anae, 138

Waikīkī, 152–153

Waikiki Beachboy (Timmons), 108

Waimea, 79, 86, 93, 114, 117

Waimea Plantation Cottages, 57–58

Wai'oli Mission, 22

water, names for, 95–96

Wilcox, Abner, 43

Wilcox, A. S., 43, 45, 48

Wilcox, Lucy, 43

Williamson, Dan, 123

winds, 140
    destruction by, 104
    names of, 121–122

windward, 96, 108, 136, 139

wood, 38, 39, 51
    as building material, 37, 114, 154, 164
    as decor, 59, 63, 76, 108, 151–153
    see also koa

Wood, Hart, 24, 26, 57

Working in Hawaii, a Labor History (Beechert), 64

Works of the People of Old, The (Kamakau), 18